TAKE-HOME

HARCOURT SCIENCE

BOOKS

Harcourt School Publishers

Orlando • Boston • Dallas • Chicago • San Diego

www.harcourtschool.com

Printed in the United States of America

ISBN 0-15-315431-4

7 8 9 10   054   2002 2001 2000

HARCOURT SCIENCE
Contents

Harcourt

About the Take-Home Books

These delightful books are designed to extend the content in the *Harcourt Science* Pupil Edition. There is one Take-Home Book for every chapter in the Pupil Edition. Although the Take-Home Books are intended to supplement *Harcourt Science,* they can also be used independently of the program.

Each Take-Home Book contains

▶ Fast Facts—high-interest facts to engage students in the topic.

▶ Feature Story—content to extend and enrich the content in the Pupil Edition chapter. This section of the book can be used to reinforce grade-level reading skills.

▶ Hands-On Activity—a science investigation students can do at home or school. Materials required for the activity are usually household items.

▶ Vocabulary Fun—puzzles and activities that provide reinforcement of the vocabulary introduced in the feature story.

▶ Science Fun—new information, puzzles, riddles, and cartoons to bring closure to each topic.

Take-Home Books are intended to be copied and sent home with students at the end of each chapter. However, you may wish to distribute the books in class and have students work on them in small groups. Some of the topics in the Take-Home Books lend themselves to further study as part of a class or individual science fair project.

The Take-Home Books provide family support. Students can take them home to read with family members. They can also involve family members in hands-on activities, vocabulary reinforcement, and science fun!

To assemble a Take-Home Book, first photocopy the master pages so that they contain the front and back side of the page, just as it appears in this book. Then, fold the pages and assemble them so the eight pages of the Take-Home Book are in order.

SPORTS MEDICINE

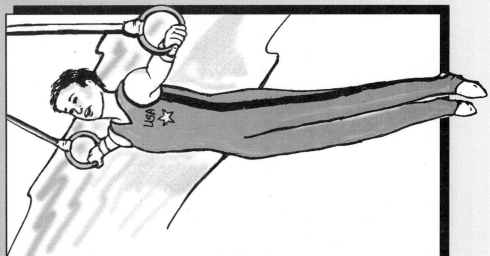

FAST FACT

Many of the more than 150,000 total hip replacements performed in the U.S. each year are due to sports injuries.

FAST FACT

Water is very therapeutic. Swimming pools are one of the best tools for sports injury rehabilitation.

FAST FACT

Today, home and gym exercise equipment has biofeedback devices that only Olympic training centers used to offer.

Fold

Science Fun

RIDDLES FOR YOUR FUNNY BONE!

▲ 1. What is an orthopedic doctor's favorite candy?
▲ 2. What do you call a picture of an athlete with a broken arm?
▲ 3. What is a crutch's favorite song?
▲ 4. What dance do ankles hate?
▲ 5. At the end of a game, where do you find athletes who forgot to stretch?
▲ 6. What proves your constitutional right to have your cast removed?

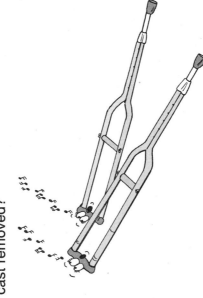

Read more about sports medicine:

Chance of a Lifetime by Melissa Lowell
A Risky Prescription: Sports and Health by Sandy Stiefer

Answers to Vocabulary Fun: 1. replacement, 2. physical therapist, 3. pulse, 4. swollen,
5. surgery, 6. specialist, 7. muscle, 8. Lange Scale.

Answers to Science Fun: 1. liga-mints (ligaments), 2. a sling shot, 3. "Lean on Me," 4. the twist,
5. on a stretcher, 6. the right to bare arms.

SPORTS INJURY

You don't have to be an athlete to benefit from the science of sports medicine. However, you can thank athletes for many breakthroughs in curing injuries to joints, bones, muscles, ligaments, and tendons. When athletes are injured, they need to be healthy and active again as soon as possible. This has caused doctors and other medical researchers to develop new ways to help athletes' injuries heal faster. These developments are eventually passed along to benefit the rest of us.

Down for the Count

The most common sports injuries involve the joints—knees, ankles, feet, fingers, wrists, elbows, shoulders, neck, and back. Of all our body parts, joints have the most stress due to weight, twisting, and impact. Athletes usually experience acute injuries involving torn ligaments. Non-athletes tend to get overuse injuries from using the same muscle groups over and over.

Find Out

Do you have a favorite sports figure? Find out what kind of injuries he or she has had. How were these injuries treated?

Fold

Vocabulary Fun

E Is for Exercise

For the following missing words, the E's have been filled in for you. Figure out each word with the help of the clues given.

1. Not the original, as in a hip ___ E ___ ___ ___ E ___ E ___

2. A specialist who may be called in to help after surgery
   ___ ___ ___ E ___ E ___

3. Is faster after strenuous exercise ___ ___ ___ ___ E ___

4. Larger than normal; puffy ___ ___ ___ E ___

5. Another word for *operation* ___ ___ ___ E ___

6. A doctor who studies a certain thing
   ___ ___ E ___ ___ ___ ___

7. Tough elastic tissue that makes body parts move
   ___ ___ E ___

8. Used to rank the seriousness of an athlete's injury
   ___ ___ E ___ ___ E ___

EXERCISE AND YOUR HEART

Your pulse rate increases during aerobic exercise. Try it for yourself and see.

MATERIALS

▶ running shoes ▶ stop watch ▶ pencil ▶ paper

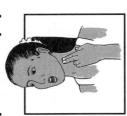

PROCEDURE

Find your pulse, either on your neck or wrist, and measure it while you are at rest, before you get out of bed, for one minute. Write it down. Now, make your bed. Time your rate again for one minute. How fast is it now? Then walk the length of one city block. Run up and down some stairs. What is your pulse rate after each of these activities? Think of other activities to do, and see how they affect your pulse rate. Be sure to wait for your pulse rate to return to its resting rate each time before starting a new test activity.

CONCLUSIONS

How do different activities affect your heart rate? Does your heart rate change after you eat breakfast or do the dishes?

Find out more about heart rates in general. How many times does an elephant's heart beat per minute? What about a hummingbird's heart?

THE LANGE SCALE

Sports medicine specialists rank an athlete's injury using the Lange Scale, which goes from 1 to 10. Anything below a 4 can usually be self-treated by relaxing training schedules or doing cross-training exercises until the pain is gone. An injury ranked above a 4 may require more serious treatment.

Doctor, Doctor!

There are several different kinds of sports injury specialists. **Primary-care sports medicine specialists** diagnose and treat athletic injuries and conditions. They decide whom the athlete needs to see next. They might recommend one or more of the following specialists:

- a **podiatrist**, who specializes in injuries stemming from poor posture or poor gait—that is, how you walk and run.

- an **orthopedic surgeon**, who performs surgeries on joints and bones.

- a **chiropractor**, who relieves spinal pain and helps athletes keep their bodies in balance.

- a **physical therapist**, who helps rehabilitate an athlete with exercise and other therapies after he or she has undergone surgery or other treatments.

— Fold —

PASS THE ICE, PLEASE

Common treatments athletes use after an injury include the following:

- ice packs—reduce swelling and help muscles recover.
- heat therapy—increases blood flow to the injured area.
- electric stimulation—increases blood flow, reduces swelling, increases mobility of the injured area, and strengthens injured muscles.
- iontophoresis—introduces ionized drugs through the skin using direct electric current.
- whirlpool baths—improve circulation and promote relaxation.

WHAT'S NEW?

Only a decade ago, knee surgery was considered a serious operation. It could take 8 to 10 weeks to recover from knee surgery. Today, arthroscopic surgery uses a tiny TV camera attached to flexible strands of glass that produce bright fiber-optic light. There is an eyepiece attached to the outside of the tube. The surgeon can operate in the tiniest places of the body without making more then a Band-Aid-sized incision, or cut. The best part is that it only takes a couple of days to recover from this type of operation.

Fold

AN AMERICAN HERO

Gymnast Shannon Miller was only a couple of months away from the biggest competition of her young life during the 1992 Summer Olympics in Barcelona, Spain. While practicing on the uneven bars one day, she fractured and dislocated her elbow, chipping the bone. This type of injury can take at least 3 to 6 months to heal, but Shannon was lucky. Her doctor decided to operate immediately and was able to screw the bone chip back to her bone, stabilizing her elbow and allowing her free use of her arm. Not long after the operation, Shannon walked away with an Olympic silver medal!

Think & Do

On a sheet of paper, design a brand-new piece of high-tech exercise equipment. What is it designed to do? What will it be able to measure? What will you call this piece of equipment? What types of athletes would benefit most from your new invention?

HELPER DOGS

Fold

German shepherds served as messengers and guards in World War I. They also helped search for and find enemy soldiers and performed rescue work for the Red Cross.

FAST FACT
Napoleon Bonaparte was rescued by a Newfoundland after falling out of a boat while trying to escape exile.

FAST FACT
Some dogs have even been trained to help people having seizures. These dogs alert others that the patient is having a seizure, sometimes by activating an emergency medical signal.

Take-Home Book • 1

Harcourt

Science Fun

That Darn Cat!

Elsa, a woman in San Diego who is blind, trained her cat, Rhubarb, to be a Seeing Eye cat. When Elsa is outside and the telephone rings, Rhubarb fetches her and guides her to the phone!

QUESTION AND ANSWER TIME

▲ Q: How are guard dogs like trees?
A: *Both use their bark for protection.*

▲ Q: Why did the ranch dog get a driver's license?
A: *He knew there was a cattle drive coming up.*

▲ Q: What did the Seeing Eye dog say to show his loyalty?
A: *I only have eyes for you.*

Answers to Vocabulary Fun: Answers will vary. 1. alert others that the owner is having a seizure, 2. sniff and search for the drugs, bark to alert owner, 3. guide the owner as he or she walks, crosses a street, avoids low tree limbs, 4. pull a wheelchair, turn on a computer, switch off and on lights, 5. listen for phone or door bell ringing, and alert owner by touch, 6. round up the animals, listening to orders communicated by whistles, 7. search, find, and bark to alert search team.

8 • Take-Home Book

SEEING EYE DOGS
TAKE THE LEAD

Some dogs are highly trained to help people who are blind. Perhaps you know someone who has a Seeing Eye dog. They are trained to help visually impaired people cross streets, climb stairs, and walk safely down busy streets. They are taught to stop at curbs, to avoid tree limbs overhead, and to avoid bicycles and other dangers at ground level.

Did you know that Seeing Eye dogs are trained to *disobey* if their master gives a command that would lead him or her into danger? At a street crossing, a Seeing Eye dog will not go forward, even if commanded, if it is not safe to cross.

These dogs spend the first year of their lives in foster homes, where they learn basic obedience. Then they work with a personal trainer for 3 to 6 months, learning commands like *left*, *right*, and *halt*. Special harnesses allow them to guide their masters. When the harness is taken off at the end of the day, the dogs know it's time to play and relax.

— Fold —

VocabularyFun

Dogs are smart, loving, and loyal to their owners. No wonder they are called our best friend! They were the first animal to be tamed and later trained to help people in many ways.

Listed below are problems that people experience. On the line, write the solution that trained dogs bring to their owners.

1. epileptic seizure: _____

2. illegal drugs: _____

3. impaired vision: _____

4. physical handicap: _____

5. impaired hearing: _____

6. scattered herds of livestock: _____

7. lost or missing people: _____

Answers on page 8

Harcourt

Good Dog!

Dogs are also trained to help people who cannot speak, hear, or use their arms and legs. These dogs are trained to open doors, flip light switches on and off, retrieve objects, and give important messages to their masters by barking and whining. These dogs pull wheelchairs and even turn on computers.

Dogs have a keen sense of hearing. They can hear high-pitched sounds that people cannot hear. They also can hear and distinguish familiar sounds at great distances.

Some Hearing Ear dogs can understand 260 sign language hand signals. They help their deaf masters by alerting them when the phone or doorbell rings, the alarm clock goes off, the smoke alarm sounds, or the baby cries.

Think & Do

For a short time, close your eyes and have a friend lead you around your house or the neighborhood. How much do you rely on your friend? Now trade places. What obstacles must you alert your friend to?

— Fold —

YOUR SENSE OF SMELL

Our sense of smell is very important to us. For one thing, it helps us taste food.

MATERIALS

- grater
- peeled raw potato
- peeled apple
- lemon rind
- peeled raw onion
- paper towel
- 4 spoons
- plate
- blindfold
- glass of water
- notebook and pencil
- plastic wrap

PROCEDURE

Wash your hands. Grate each food item onto a paper towel, washing the grater after each one. Put $\frac{1}{4}$ teaspoon of each food on the plate and cover it. Blindfold a friend. Have your friend pinch his or her nose and taste each food, washing his or her mouth out with a sip of water after each one. Tell your friend to let the food linger on the tongue and not to chew. Wait one minute and then ask your friend to identify the food. Write down the responses.

CONCLUSIONS

Was your friend able to identify the foods correctly? How important is our sense of smell when it comes to eating?

LEADERS OF THE PACK

For thousands of years, farmers have used dogs to help around the farm. For centuries, dogs have been bred to herd sheep and guard corrals or flocks. In some countries, dogs even pull carts of vegetables to market.

Herding dogs can control large numbers of livestock that are much bigger than they are! How do they do it? They circle the sheep or cattle, gathering them in, while staring them straight in the eye. Sometimes they show them who's boss by barking. If one strays, the dog chases it back to the group. The farmer uses a series of whistles to communicate with the dog.

Farmers also need dogs to help them protect their livestock. Great Pyrenees, komondors, and several other breeds are fierce and smart enough for this important job. But, believe it or not, donkeys and llamas also make effective farm guards!

POWERFUL SENSE OF SMELL

Dogs have a powerful sense of smell. Where people recognize things by sight, dogs use smell instead. A dog keeps its nose wet by licking it. A gland inside the nose also helps keep it moist. This wetness helps dogs detect odors, including some that people can't smell at all. Specially trained dogs are sometimes brought in to sniff out dangerous gas leaks in buildings.

Dogs can sniff clothes and pick the ones that were worn, or even touched, by a particular person. This makes them valuable in searching for missing persons. They have found and dragged people from burning buildings, rescued earthquake and avalanche victims under piles of rock or snow, and saved people from drowning. One famous Saint Bernard named Barry rescued 40 people lost in the snow in the Saint Bernard Pass area of Switzerland around 1800.

Find Out

Did you know that dogs are taken into some nursing homes and hospitals to cheer up patients? These animals provide love and companionship, and even some licks! Learn more about animal therapy programs in your area and how you can get involved.

GIANT COASTAL REDWOODS

Nevada

California

Location of coastal redwoods

FAST FACT

Fossil redwoods, with the oldest more than 160 million years old, have been found along coastal regions of the United States, Canada, Europe, and Asia.

FAST FACT

The cutting down of California redwoods began in 1860. At that time there were 2 million redwoods. Today, only about 4.5 percent of the old-growth trees remain.

FAST FACT

A coastal redwood in northern California is said to be the world's tallest tree. It is about 112 m (367 ft) high.

Take-Home Book • 1

Fold

Harcourt

Science Fun

RIDDLE ME

▲ Q: What makes redwoods such good sports fans?

A: *They love to root.*

▲ Q: Why do redwoods sleep so soundly?

A: *They're in a fo-rest.*

▲ Q: What do some pick-up trucks and redwoods have in common?

A: *They both have canopies.*

▲ Q: Why are redwoods so good at brainstorming?

A: *They know how to branch out.*

▲ Q: Why can't redwoods sew?

A: *They lose too many needles.*

Old-Timers

Write a story from the point of view of a giant coastal redwood. Describe how this old-timer feels, and what it has experienced and seen in its long life. Who knows, it might even be a tall tale!

WIN!

Go Team!

Answers to Vocabulary Fun: Across: 1. tannin, 2. sapling, 3. resistant, 4. nutrients, 5. canopy, 6. giant redwoods; Down: 7. heartwood, 8. insulate, 9. sapwood, 10. cambium

8 • Take-Home Book

Unit A • Chapter 3 TH9

THE WORLD'S OLDEST TREES

Have you ever been in a redwood forest? Many trees are over 20 stories tall. They are bigger around than giant-sized banquet tables. The air is moist from the plentiful rainfall and Pacific Ocean fog. The sunlight finds its way through the boughs.

The Life of a Redwood

As redwoods grow, their shallow roots spread far out under the forest floor. Their bark grows thicker, protecting the

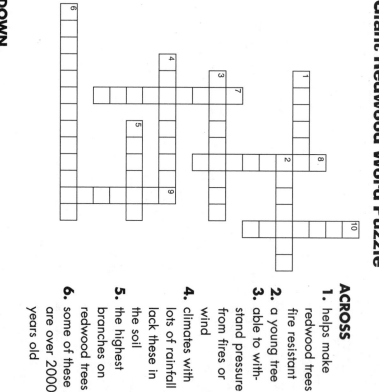

BARK
SAPWOOD
HEARTWOOD
CAMBIUM LAYER

cambium, a thin layer of cells. The cambium adds a new layer of bark each year and a new layer of wood called the *sapwood.* The oldest sapwood becomes the *heartwood.* The heartwood is in the center of the trunk and helps the tree stand straight and tall.

Find Out

Why is redwood such a prized wood? What is it used for? What other materials could be used in place of redwood?

Vocabulary Fun

Giant Redwood Word Puzzle

ACROSS
1. helps make redwood trees fire resistant
2. a young tree
3. able to withstand pressure from fires or wind
4. climates with lots of rainfall lack these in the soil
5. the highest branches on redwood trees
6. some of these are over 2000 years old

DOWN
7. the oldest sapwood; helps trees stand straight and tall
8. to protect, as from fires
9. a new layer of wood
10. a thin layer of cells

Answers on page 8

Fold

TREE GROWTH

You probably know that circumference is the distance around something—in this case, a tree trunk. A tree's circumference is usually measured 1.5 m (about 5 ft) up from the ground.

MATERIALS

▲ tape measure
▲ a partner
▲ a small notebook and pencil
▲ field guide of trees for your area

PROCEDURE

Use your tape measure to find the point for measuring circumference. Then, have a friend hold the end of the tape measure at that point while you wrap it around the trunk. This number is the circumference of the tree. Write down your measurement. Use the tree guide to determine the kind of tree. The circumference of most mature trees increases by about 2.5 cm (1 in.) every year. Using your math skills, determine what the circumference of the tree will be in ten years and in twenty years.

CONCLUSIONS

What are some things that could slow down the tree's growth? What weather conditions could help it to grow faster?

Fold

REDWOODS AND FIRE

Redwoods are named for the color of their bark and wood. The high *tannin* content in the wood of these trees makes them highly resistant to fire. The soft, spongy bark can be up to 70 cm (about 2 ft) thick and has an even higher tannin content. The bark helps insulate and protect redwoods from fires. Burn scars can be seen on the bark of the oldest trees.

A 2000-year-old tree may have felt the searing heat of more than 100 fires in its lifetime, but it continues to grow and reproduce. Fires even help redwoods reproduce by

• drying the trees' cones so they release their seeds onto the ground.
• sterilizing the soil so seedlings can survive and thrive.
• covering the ground with a thin layer of ash that helps seedlings grow.
• clearing the forest floor of smaller trees and plants.
• making openings in the forest canopy so sunlight can filter through.

DELICATE ROOTS

Redwoods have very shallow root systems that may extend 20 to 25 m (about 65 to 80 ft) out from the tree. National and state parks have built trails that help protect the redwoods by keeping people from tramping over their delicate roots. Sometimes redwood roots send root crown sprouts up through the ground. They encircle the tree in what is called a *fairy circle* of new trees.

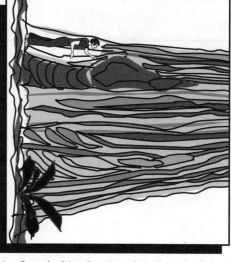

The Perfect Recycling System

Like soil in other high-rainfall areas, the California coastal redwood forest soil has few nutrients. Most of the nutrients necessary for life are found in the trees, both living and dead, and in other forest plants and animals. When trees are removed from the forest, many nutrients are lost.

LIFE IN THE REDWOOD FOREST

What else lives in redwood forests? You may be lucky to see a herd of elk in coastal redwood forests. There are also skunks, raccoons, black bears, deer, porcupines, weasels, and even rare ring-tailed cats. The marbled murrelet and the northern spotted owl both nest in old-growth forests.

Save-the-Redwoods League

Since 1918, the Save-the-Redwoods League (SRL) has worked to protect coastal redwood forests by buying lands for the California Redwood State Park and Redwood National Park. It is hoped that once they are protected, the redwoods' natural ability to survive and endure will enable them to flourish and grow for many more thousands of years.

Think & Do

Make an illustrated time line that shows what Redwoods have lived through in their lives.

FLOWER SHAPES

How Flowers and Bees Work Together

FAST FACT
Bees see most of the colors we do, but they don't see red, which looks like black to them. They do see one color that we can't—ultraviolet.

FAST FACT
Honeybees can identify a flavor as sweet, sour, salty, or bitter.

FAST FACT
The shape of a periwinkle's flower is designed so only the best pollinator can reach its nectar. A bee's tongue, but not an ant's body, can fit down the narrow throat of this flower.

— Fold —

Harcourt

Science Fun

Did You Know . . .
The dishonest bog orchid attracts bees with false promises of food. It has fake nectar guides that lead to nectar that doesn't exist.

Did You Know . . .
A butterfly also has a proboscis. The butterfly uses it to suck nectar. When it's not in use, the butterfly rolls the proboscis up under its head to keep it out of the way.

BEE RIDDLES

▲ Q: Why don't bees peek into ants' nests?
A: *They figure it's none of their bees-ness.*

▲ Q: What male singer do bees like best?
A: *Sting*

▲ Q: Why don't bees have hobbies?
A: *They are too buzzy.*

Answer to Vocabulary Fun: Bees pollinate flowers.

PLANTS + INSECTS = BEST FRIENDS FOREVER

For plants to continue to exist, they have to make new plants. To do this, flowering plants need to be pollinated. Insects are one of their best helpers. A flower's nectar, shape, color, scent, texture, and opening and closing all help it reproduce.

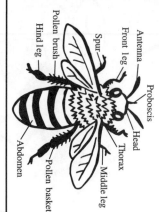

Antenna
Front leg
Spur
Pollen brush
Hind leg
Pollen basket
Proboscis
Head
Thorax
Middle leg
Pollen basket
Abdomen

Bees are very important pollinators. A bee's body is designed to gather pollen. Pollen sticks to the fine hairs on the bee's head, thorax, and abdomen. Antennae help a bee feel its way inside flowers. A bee's hind legs have broad, hollowed-out parts that become tiny baskets to carry pollen. Combs on the other four legs help brush the pollen from the bee's body and pack it into the baskets. A bee's 19-mm (about $\frac{3}{4}$-in.) tongue is a long tube on the outside of its head. This strawlike tube is called a *proboscis* (proh•BAHS•is).

Empty pollen basket

Full pollen basket

Fold

Harcourt

Vocabulary Fun

Fill in the missing letters in the following sentences.

1. __ees cannot see red.
   1

2. Some __lo__ers need insec__s for pollination.
   11 12   10

3. Flowering __lants need poll__n to reproduce.
   4   2

4. Color attracts bees to the Spa__ish bro__m.
   8   5

5. Lines on the __ris point the way to pollen.
   7

6. Some of the f__owers use odo__ to attract insects.
   6   13

7. A flower's __hape protects its nect__r.
   3   9

Now fill in the letters above the matching numbers below.
Read the hidden message.

__ __ __   __ __ __ __ __ __ __ __ __ __
1 2 3   4 5 6 6 7 8 9 10 2

__ __ __ __ __ __ __ __ .
11 6 5 12 2 13 3

Answers on page 8

ALL IN A DAY'S WORK

Insects are attracted to flowers. For example, the flower of the bright yellow Spanish broom draws bees by its color. Then it gives bees a landing place on its broad lower petals. Once landed, the bees move further inside the flower to look for nectar, a sticky sweet liquid the flower produces for animals and insects. As the bee climbs in, the flower's anthers curl back and dust the bee with pollen.

Nectar Guides When flowers first appeared on Earth, they had very simple shapes. As flowers began to produce nectar, their shapes evolved to store, protect, and advertise it. In ancient flowers, nectar was easy to find. Now, nectar is often well hidden so only good pollinators can find it. It is protected from rain and wind. The lines of an iris, a pansy's "face," and a petunia's star shape all point the way to nectar.

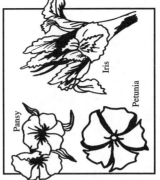

Pansy

Iris

Petunia

Find Out

Investigate some flowers. Look carefully at their shapes and colors. Can you find ways that flowers use shape and color to lure insects to their nectar?

Take-Home Book • 3

— Fold —

SEARCHING FOR FLOWERS

Scientists learn a lot by observation. Keep a record of flowers in your area.

MATERIALS

▶ **drawing book that will become your field journal**
▶ **pencil**   ▶ **colored pencils**   ▶ **hand lens**

PROCEDURE

1. In your field journal, keep a record of the flowers in your area. Make a drawing of each one. If there are no flowers in bloom at this time in the area where you live, use a plant magazine or book.

2. Take time to look carefully at the color, shape, size, and structure of the flowers. Do they have a scent? Sit quietly and observe each one awhile. What visits each flower? Can you identify each flower's nectar guide? Make some notes.

3. Look at a flower and some pollen with your hand lens. What do you see now that you missed before?

CONCLUSIONS

If you do not notice any insects on a particular flowering plant, try to guess which kinds of insects might pollinate this plant. What clues does the flower give you?

6 • Take-Home Book

FLOWER SHAPES

A flower's shape can make it easy or extremely difficult for insects to find the nectar and pollen. Some shapes are even customized for particular insects.

- The comfrey's bell shape protects its pollen and nectar.
- Small tube shapes are made for bees to reach or crawl into to get the nectar. Many tube flowers are blue.
- Some flowers, like red clover, have tightly closed petals. Such flowers can only be entered by very strong insects such as bumblebees, who can pry apart the flower's petals.
- Snapdragons have little mouths. See for yourself how snapdragons work! Put your finger in the mouth of a snapdragon. (Make sure there isn't a bee inside!) When you remove your finger, the side that corresponds to a bee's back will have the most pollen.

Wanted: Bumblebees

When red clover was introduced into New Zealand, the plant did not produce any seeds, because New Zealand had no native bumblebees to pollinate the clover. After bumblebees were imported, farmers could successfully grow clover.

Fold

PLAYING ROUGH

Some flowers don't mess around! The flowers on the Scotch broom plant fire pollen at insects in small explosions. Another species tempts visitors with drops of nectar on its petals. The insects fall into a pool and pick up pollen as they try to escape with their lives.

Still other flowers trap insects, such as some flies and beetles, until pollination happens. Plants like the spotted arum send out the odor of spoiled meat. Flies are attracted and pass down through the hairs to the base of the flower. When they try to leave, their way is blocked by the hairs, which go the other way. Once they finally manage to leave, they are well-dusted with pollen.

Think & Do

Design a new flower shape or other device to get a certain type of insect to enter and leave after being covered with pollen. Label the parts of your flower, and describe the process the insect uses to enter and leave it.

Harcourt

DRY AS A BONE

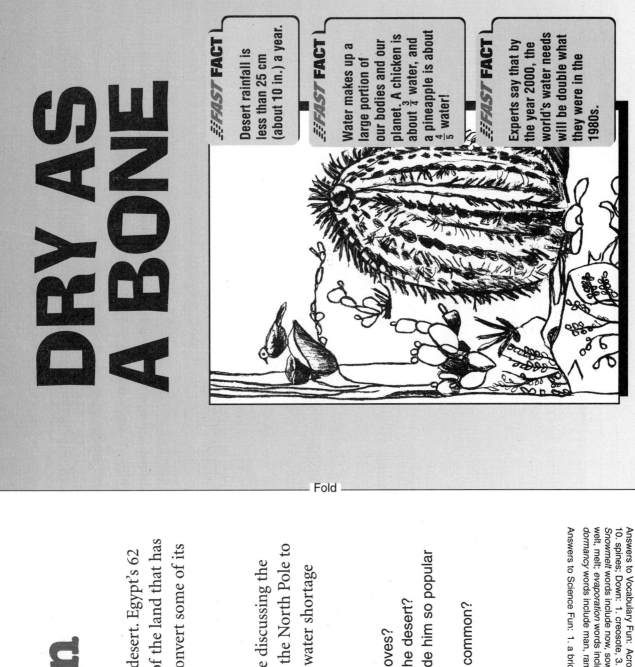

FAST FACT

Desert rainfall is less than 25 cm (about 10 in.) a year.

FAST FACT

Water makes up a large portion of our bodies and our planet. A chicken is about $\frac{3}{4}$ water, and a pineapple is about $\frac{4}{5}$ water!

FAST FACT

Experts say that by the year 2000, the world's water needs will be double what they were in the 1980s.

Fold

Harcourt

Science Fun

CLOSE QUARTERS

In Egypt, 95 percent of the land is desert. Egypt's 62 million people live on the 5 percent of the land that has water. Research how Egypt plans to convert some of its desert land into farmland.

Stay Tuned!

In San Diego, California, people are discussing the possibility of towing an iceberg from the North Pole to southern California to help solve the water shortage problem.

RIDDLES

▲ 1. What crosses a river but never moves?

▲ 2. What is the most popular fruit in the desert?

▲ 3. What did the king predict that made him so popular in Tucson?

▲ 4. What do cacti and books have in common?

Answers to Vocabulary Fun: Across: 2. reservoir, 5. camanchaca, 7. seeds, 8. water, 10. spines; Down: 1. creosote, 3. glacier, 4. cacti, 6. pineapples, 9. rainfall. *Snowmelt* words include now, sow, mow, low, tow, melt, slow, smelt, snow, mole, sole, molt, welt, melt; *evaporation* words include neat, ate, rate, rain, ear, near, ration, tire, note, poor, vat; *dormancy* words include man, ram, can, roam, corn, road, cord, or, dam, ran, norm.

Answers to Science Fun: 1. a bridge, 2. watermelon, 3. a long reign (rain), 4. their spines

COOL WATER

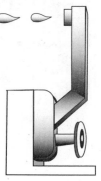

Feeling thirsty? If you're like a lot of people, you probably just turn the faucet on. But do you know where your drinking water comes from? In most cases, cities and towns get their water from rivers, lakes, or reservoirs that collect rainfall and snowmelt. There are also vast underground sources of water. Water treatment plants clean the water and make it safe for drinking.

In some dry places, like Tucson, Arizona, the underground water supply is being used up faster than nature can replace it. In such a hot, desert climate, summer temperatures can reach 55°C (about 130°F). A day without water in that blazing sun can cause death.

Desert Dwellers

Hundreds of years ago, Native Americans built canals leading from mountain reservoirs that still supply much of Arizona's irrigation water. But Arizona needs and uses more water than it can get from streams and storage reservoirs. Several large-scale projects have made it possible to harness water from the Colorado River. Residents of Arizona now have as much water as people who live in areas that get 50 cm (about 20 in.) of rain a year.

Harcourt

Vocabulary Fun

On the Subject of Water

ACROSS

2. used to collect rainfall and snowmelt

5. Chilean fog

7. they can be very patient

8. a precious resource

10. the pointy tips of cacti

DOWN

1. its leaves are coated with wax

3. an estimated 97 percent of fresh water is trapped here

4. cattle will eat them if hungry or thirsty enough

6. these are $\frac{4}{5}$ water

9. lacking in desert regions

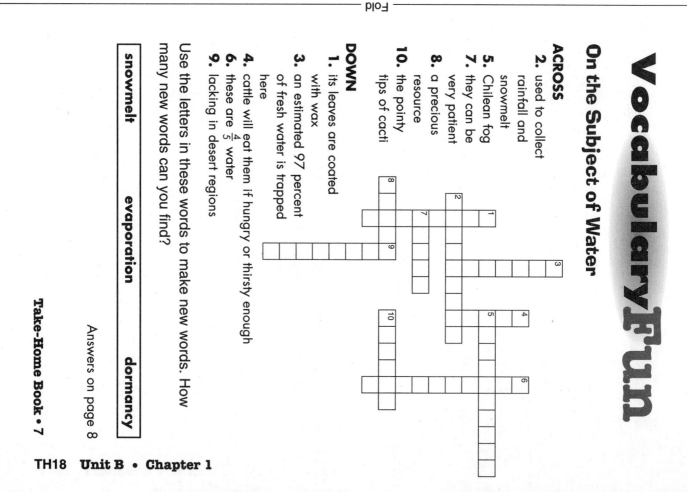

Use the letters in these words to make new words. How many new words can you find?

snowmelt	evaporation	dormancy

Answers on page 8

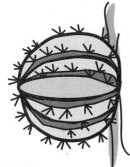

SMART PLANTS

In Tucson, plants have found ways to survive with very little water. They can go into a kind of sleep, or dormancy. The leaves of the creosote bush, for example, are coated with wax. This wax keeps water from evaporating during long dry spells. The plant looks brown and dead until a rainstorm. Then new branches and leaves quickly sprout.

Some plants in Tucson and in other dry areas survive by storing water. The most famous of these plants is the cactus. Like an accordion, a cactus stem expands and contracts to hold varying amounts of water. Cacti also have shallow roots that absorb even small amounts of water from the ground. When it rains, they quickly grow tiny extra roots in order to absorb water as fast as possible before it evaporates!

Think & Do

What plants might you suggest planting in Tucson, Arizona? Why? Draw a diagram of a yard landscaped with the plants you would choose. What kind of plants would grow best in your area? Why is it good to landscape with an area's geography and climate in mind?

Take-Home Book • 3

— Fold —

Harcourt

STAYING ALIVE

What would you do if you got lost in a desert and ran out of water? Here's a way to get water out of the atmosphere, even in the Sahara.

MATERIALS

▲ small shovel
▲ cup
▲ some leaves
▲ piece of plastic
▲ 3 or 4 rocks

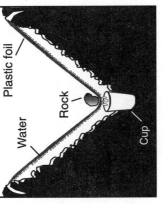

Plastic foil

Rock

Water

Cup

PROCEDURE

Dig a hole bigger than your cup, and put your cup in it. Put the leaves in the hole around the base of the cup. Poke a small hole in the middle of the plastic, and place it over the entire hole. Use the rocks to secure the edges of the plastic, and put one small rock in the middle near the hole to form a slope. Leave the setup overnight, and in the morning you'll have water in the cup!

CONCLUSIONS

Where do you think the water in the cup came from? How do you think the plant leaves helped get water? Look up the word *condensation*, if necessary. What does it mean?

6 • Take-Home Book

WORTH ITS WEIGHT IN GOLD

The Atacama Desert in northern Chile gets less rainfall than anywhere else on Earth. Some parts of the Atacama have never reported rain! Until the 1970s, residents of Caleta Chungungo, a coastal village on the fringes of the Atacama, got their water from an iron mine on a 760-m (about 2500-ft) mountain ridge about 6 kilometers (4 mi) inland. When the mine closed, villagers' fresh water had to be trucked in every week from about 40 km (25 mi) away.

Forecast: *NO RAIN*

Looking Up

In this region of Chile, hot desert air sucks out all the moisture from the chilly coastal Pacific Ocean breezes. As this air moves east, away from the ocean, it encounters the high mountain ridges near Caleta Chungungo. The air has to rise to go over the ridge. As it rises, it cools down and the moisture in it condenses to form a dense fog that hugs the top of the ridge. Local Chileans call this fog the *camanchaca*.

HARNESSING CLOUDS

After seeing how the moisture from the *camanchaca* condensed on the leaves of eucalyptus trees on a nearby mountaintop, scientists decided to try to harvest this fog water—a renewable resource—for use by the entire region.

Fog for Breakfast

Large fog collectors were built on top of the mountain. Using poles and mesh screens, scientists set up huge nets to catch the fog flowing in from the ocean. It takes about ten million tiny fog droplets, caught in the net, to make one large raindrop. As the drops get bigger, gravity pulls them into a trough below. They are then moved through a gravity-fed pipeline 7 km (about 4.5 mi) down to a large reservoir in Caleta Chungungo. From there the water flows to newly installed faucets in people's homes. A solar-powered chlorination system makes sure the water is drinkable. During a dense *camanchaca*, this system could collect about 60,000 L (16,000 gal) of fog water a day, more than enough to satisfy local demand.

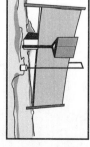

Find Out

Learn about other dry areas and the interesting ways they get water.

POLAR BEARS

and Other Things That Live in the Arctic

FAST FACT
Polar bears are powerful. As swimmers, they've been spotted in open ocean 1600 km (about 1000 mi) from shore. They can run for short bursts up to 55 km (about 35 mi) per hour.

FAST FACT
Many Arctic animals, such as the polar bear and the Arctic fox, have unusually tiny ears that lie close to their bodies to conserve heat.

FAST FACT
The *permafrost*, or area of permanently frozen ground in the Arctic, can be more than 1 km (about 0.6 mi) deep!

Fold

Harcourt

Science Fun

Why Is the Arctic Called the "White Desert"?

Even though there is water, snow, and ice everywhere, the Arctic averages only about 15 to 25 cm (about 6 to 10 in.) of rainfall a year—less than many deserts.

▲ 1. What's in this picture? *(10 polar bears, 16 snowshoe hares, 3 Arctic foxes, and 1 snowy owl, in a blizzard, of course!)*

▲ 2. What form of Arctic transportation never runs out of gas, refuses to start, or freezes up in the cold? *(sled dogs)*

WHAT A COOL BEARSKIN RUG...! I WONDER WHO LEFT IT.

Answers to Vocabulary Fun: 1. tundra; 2. permafrost; 3. a predator; 4. insulation; 5. the Arctic

BRRR . . . IT'S COLD IN THE ARCTIC!

The color and body structure of Arctic animals like the polar bear help them survive in the freezing cold.

White on White

It's no surprise that many Arctic animals, including the snowy owl, snowshoe hare, and Arctic fox, are white. Against the ice and snow, white helps protect them from predators, animals who would love to eat them.

Polar bears' white-looking fur helps them, too. They wait patiently for hours near holes in the ice for seals to appear. Sometimes polar bears flatten down and slither on their bellies across the ice to sneak up on their prey. They may even cover their black eyes and nose with a paw as they crawl, or they may push a clump of snow or ice ahead of them as a shield! When a seal appears, the polar bear takes just one swat with a powerful forepaw, and dinner is served.

Fold

VocabularyFun

| permafrost |
| the Arctic |
| a predator |
| tundra |
| insulation |

Riddles

Use the words from the vocabulary box above to answer the following riddles.

1. I am the flat land of the very cold region. I have only low-growing plants. What am I? _____

2. I am ground that is always frozen. What am I? _____

3. I am one that lives by eating prey. What am I? _____

4. I can be fat or blubber. I help keep animals warm. What am I? _____

5. I am the region of the North Pole. What am I? _____

FABULOUS FAT

Fat is a great insulator. See for yourself!

MATERIALS

▲ **2 plastic bags**

▲ **small bucket half-filled with cold water and ice cubes**

▲ **large spoon**

▲ **1 pound of shortening**

▲ **masking tape**

PROCEDURE

1. Spoon the shortening into one of the plastic bags.

2. Fill the bucket with water. Add ice cubes.

3. Put your hand in the other plastic bag. Tape it securely around your wrist. Put your hand in the water.

4. Now put your bagged hand inside the bag filled with shortening. Tape the bag around your wrist. Put your hand back in the water.

CONCLUSIONS

Does your hand feel as cold as it did before? Why or why not? What have you learned about fat as an insulator? Why is it important for people to have some fat on their bodies?

PUTTING THEIR BEST FEET FORWARD

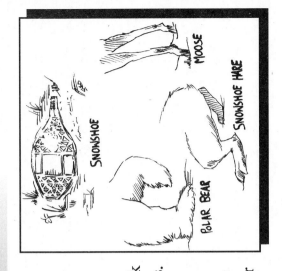

Thick fur on the soles of polar bears' feet prevents heat loss and provides traction. It also allows them to move silently, so they can sneak up on unsuspecting seals. Lemmings also have fur on the soles of their feet to help them grip the ice as they run through their underground tunnels.

Snowshoe hares have big pads of fur on their large hind feet. Their toes spread apart when they run, which prevents them from sinking deeply into the snow.

Moose, however, don't mind sinking! Their long legs are designed for wading through very deep snow. They can lift their feet straight up so high that their hooves often don't even drag across the snow!

Find Out

Put on your boots, and go walking with a family member after a heavy snow. Measure how far you sink into the snow.

INSULATION

Have you ever heard about people who have survived in severe cold by digging snow caves to keep themselves warm? Huskies—Arctic sled dogs—know about this. They dig caves in the snow the size of their bodies and curl up, using their body heat to warm the space.

Animals' thick fur provides insulation against the icy water and cold air. Arctic foxes sleep warmly by curling up in a ball and tucking their heads beneath their thick, furry tails. Polar bears have two types of fur. The white-looking outer hair acts as camouflage. The woolly, oily undercoat keeps them dry and holds in body heat.

Long ago, the Eskimos learned many things from Arctic animals. They learned to wear two pairs of pants made of caribou skin. The hoods of their parkas were lined with wolverine hair that caused any moisture that formed from their breath to drip off quickly. Their boots were often made of sealskin, with walrus-hide soles for toughness or polar-bear-hide soles for moving quietly.

HOW PLANTS SURVIVE

Some plants also have adaptations that allow them to survive in the harsh Arctic environment. Arctic plants grow low to the ground in clumps in order to trap and conserve heat. Being close to the ground also helps protect them from strong winds.

Since nutrients and water are in short supply, most Arctic plants have shallow, dense roots. They use the small amount of melted water held in the thin layer between the ground and the permafrost.

Think & Do

What inventions and ideas for walking on snow, keeping warm in cold weather, driving in snow, and protecting water pipes in cold weather are similar to adaptions you see in Arctic animals and plants? Now design a brand-new cold weather invention! Draw a picture of it, and explain how it works.

PINEY WOODS

FAST FACT

In 1981, the United Nations added the Big Thicket National Preserve to a list of 250 international biosphere reserves worldwide.

FAST FACT

Caddo Lake, the only natural lake in Texas, has over 60 km (about 40 mi) of "boat roads" that provide access to fishing spots and other points of interest.

FAST FACT

The Big Thicket National Preserve contains about 35,000 hectares (86,000 acres) of public land in the Piney Woods area of eastern Texas.

BIG THICKET **National Preserve**

Harcourt

Science Fun

Big Thicket has been called the American Ark. The last Ice Age pushed or encouraged species from four ecological systems into this very close and compact neighborhood. Roadrunners and bluebirds nest within short range of each other. There are nearly 300 species of birds that live here or migrate through. Fifty reptile species, including alligators, make their homes in the swamps and creeks. Add the mammal species, and you have an area teeming with an extraordinary variety of life that is rarely found outside a zoo.

RIDDLES

▶ **Q:** What do Texans and astronauts have in common?
　A: *They both like space.*

▶ **Q:** Why do wildflowers stand close together in Big Thicket?
　A: *They heard it's a jungle out there.*

▶ **Q:** Why can't you feel blue in Piney Woods?
　A: *Because the pines are ever-green.*

▶ **Q:** Why was Little Miss Muffet found crying in the middle of Big Thicket?
　A: *She lost her whey.*

Answers to Vocabulary Fun: 1. Jefferson, 2. Texas, 3. swamp buggies, 4. log jam, 5. carnivorous, 6. resin, 7. dynamite, 8. steamboat, 9. Big Thicket, 10. Piney Woods

PINEY WOODS— A TEXAS TREASURE

Think about the part of the state where you live. It has a certain climate and particular plants and animals that live there. If you traveled to a different part of your state, you would probably discover a very different climate and different plants and animals.

The Piney Woods region in the northeast corner of Texas is unlike any other part of this vast state. It has rolling hills, not flat land. It's green, not dry. There are tall pines, lakes, magnolia trees, and moss-draped swamps.

Big Thicket National Preserve Native Americans named this region "the Big Woods." Long ago, this forested, watery area was almost impassable. Today, you can take an open-air swamp buggy tour through the maze of inlets with Spanish moss dripping from the trees. Before the 1800s, Big Thicket covered over 1.4 million hectares (about 3.5 million acres). In 1974, Congress established the preserve to protect 35,000 unlogged hectares (about 86,450 acres).

Vocabulary Fun

Sticky Words

The resin is thick in these trees. It's so thick, in fact, that the letters in the words to this puzzle are all sticking together. Can you figure out each word?

1. _____   6. _____
2. _____   7. _____
3. _____   8. _____
4. _____   9. _____
5. _____   10. _____

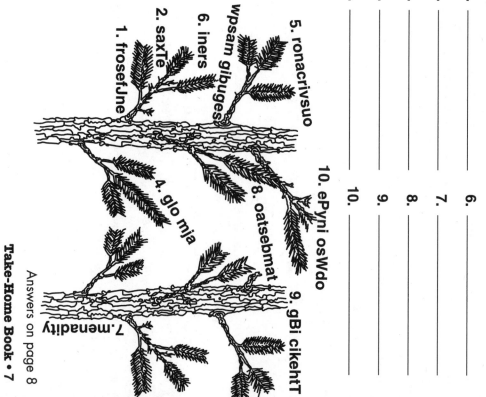

1. frosefJne
2. saxTe
3. wpsam gibuges
4. glo mja
5. ronacrivsuo
6. iners
7. menadlty
8. oatsebmat
9. gBi cikehtT
10. ePyni osWdo

Answers on page 8

Harcourt

BIG THICKET'S INCREDIBLE WOOD

Before the 1900s, the beginning of the logging industry in the area, Big Thicket was filled with longleaf pines. After 50 years of logging, the only trees left were in the area now protected by the preserve. That's the only place you can still see these beautiful trees.

These ancient pines produced lumber as tough as hardwood. They were full of resin, a sticky, yellow plant secretion. The resin protected the wood so well that longleaf pine boards could be out in the weather for many years with no protective paint on them and they would still not rot.

During the years of the logging industry, many longleaf pine logs sank to the bottom of the rivers and swamps. Now these logs are being brought to the surface and dried out. Despite 50 years of being in the water, they are not rotten. The high resin content protected the wood. These logs now provide good lumber.

— Fold —

THE FINE ART OF PRESERVATION

What happens to wood when it isn't preserved?

PROCEDURE

1. Look around your backyard or neighborhood. Can you find some unpainted wood that has been on the ground for a while? Look closely. What happened to it? How does it feel? Is anything living in it? Draw a picture of it.

2. Now look for a painted piece of wood. Observe it as you did the first piece.

3. Which piece of wood do you think would need preserving the most, one used as a cupboard shelf or one used as part of an outside deck? Why? What rots wood?

4. Do what scientists do—carry out a long-term experiment. Get two small pieces of the same kind of untreated lumber. Paint one with a couple of coats of paint to seal the wood. Leave the other one unpainted.

5. Put both pieces outside on the dirt or grass. Leave them for several months where water and sun will hit them. Observe them each month. Write down your observations in a journal.

CONCLUSIONS

How do you think resin helps to preserve the wood in Big Thicket?

NORTH AMERICA'S BEST ECOLOGY LAB

The eastern Appalachian forests, southeast swamps, Midwest prairies, and southwest deserts all come together in Big Thicket to produce an unusually high number of ecological zones. Nearly 100 soil types and 140 to 150 cm (about 55 to 60 in.) of rainfall a year combine to support 8 vegetation zones, 85 tree species, about 1000 different flowering plants, and over 300 bird species! In some places, Big Thicket has a six-layer canopy of trees. Because of this, it has been called the best-equipped ecological lab in North America.

▼ **Sundew**

Carnivorous Plants

Big Thicket also has four of the five known types of carnivorous plants found in the U.S.! Carnivorous plants trap insects for food. They are usually found in moist places, where the plants don't get enough minerals from the soil. The sundew, for example, has sticky globs at its base that shine like drops of dew. The globs attract insects and then trap them while the plant digests them.

Harcourt

THE PORT OF JEFFERSON

In the mid-1800s, Jefferson was a major inland port, thanks to a 120-km (about 75-mi) logjam of downed trees, silt, and brush that blocked the Red River's original route from Louisiana. Because of the jam, the river made a new channel, filling Caddo Lake and running over into the Big Cypress Bayou that flowed through Jefferson, Texas. The town boomed! Steamboats carried settlers, supplies, and crops, including cotton, back and forth from New Orleans. In 1872, as many as 226 steamboats landed in Jefferson. Life was good.

The End of Jefferson

Everything changed in 1873, when Army engineers used dynamite to clear the logjam. As the water returned to its normal channel, steamboats could no longer get to Jefferson. Not long after the relocation of the river's channel, the city began to change. Without a railroad or an inland port, the town's population went from 10,000 to 2000 within a few years.

SAVING WILDFLOWERS

The Goal of the Lady Bird Johnson Wildflower Center

Fold

Harcourt

Science Fun

Traveling Seeds

Seeds have very clever ways of getting around. In fact, seeds are shaped for travel. Take a walk through a field. What kinds of seeds catch a ride on your socks? How do dandelions travel? Have you ever seen a maple seed, called a *samara*? It looks just like an airplane wing. How do you think samaras might travel? What other ways do seeds travel? Make a clever poster to show how different seeds are designed for travel.

FLOWER FUN

▲ Q: What do daisies and bicycles have in common?
A: *They both have petals (pedals).*

▲ Q: What did the grandma dandelion say to her grandson?
A: *Honey, you're growing like a weed!*

▲ Q: What kind of wildflowers do you find in space?
A: *Sunflowers.*

▲ Q: Why does a rose have thorns?
A: *It wants to make a point.*

THERE'S NO PLACE LIKE HOME

Have you ever heard the expression *There's no place like home?* Just like people, native plants come from a particular place. They were not brought there by humans. Each region has its own native plants, and like a home, it is the place where they are most comfortable.

Native plants don't need much help to grow in their natural home. The soil, climate, other plants, and animals of that area are just right for them. It takes more money, water, energy, and chemicals to keep nonnative plants growing in an area. For example, to keep a lawn bright green during a dry summer takes a lot of water and fertilizer.

Native wildflowers, grasses, shrubs, and trees provide food and shelter for animals and sometimes for humans. They help keep the ecosystem of an area stable. They filter the air and reduce soil erosion.

Vocabulary Fun

Wildflower Search

Circle the names of these wildflowers in the puzzle that follows.

bluebell	aster	bluebonnet	coneflower
lupine	Iceland poppy	daisy	sage
foxglove	phlox	toadflax	mint
cosmos	chicory	grass	milkweed
larkspur	gentian	tidy tips	paintbrush
wallflower	catchfly	clover	

```
b l u e b o n n e t s a g e d
l s m i n t r c h i c o r y a
u u a c y e l t g r a s s i
e o p w v e r o b e n c a b s
b r e i c e l a n d p o p p y
e a t h n b a d y b n l u r
e a s t e r f l o e w f l
l c a t c h f l y e r f p o a
c o s m o s r a l p h l o x r
n a i t n e g x m o s o e g k
m i l k w e e d f i v w e l s
p a i n t b r u s h s e p o p
o t w a l l f l o w e r s v u
t i d y t i p s x c l o v e r
```

PRESERVATION BEGINS AT HOME

Ask your parents if you can plant a small wildflower garden.

MATERIALS

▲ small plot of land or pot   ▲ watering can

▲ wildflower seeds   ▲ rake

PROCEDURE

1. Work with your family to choose a small area for a wildflower garden. Select the kind of wildflowers you want to plant. Don't forget native grasses.

2. Clear and rake the area for your garden.

3. When scattering the seeds, remember to place them on the ground. Gently tap them down with your foot. Water lightly.

4. Take notes, and make drawings of your garden.

CONCLUSIONS

Which plants grew and which didn't? What birds and butterflies visited your garden? Enjoy your wildflower meadow!

Fold

LADY BIRD JOHNSON WILDFLOWER CENTER

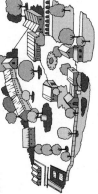

To save species of plants and animals, we need to save enough of their environment. This is especially true for wildflowers. This is the goal of the Lady Bird Johnson Wildflower Center near Austin, Texas. It was started in 1982 by Lady Bird Johnson, the widow of former President Lyndon Johnson, and by actress Helen Hayes.

Education Center

The center's goal is to "educate people on the environmental necessity, the economic value, and the natural beauty of native plants." The center's beautiful gardens help people see the beauty of native plants. The objective is to convince people to replace lawns and any nonnative plants that need a lot of water and fertilizer with native plants.

Information Center

Every year, the center's botanists answer more than 8000 requests for information about native plant species. The center is a resource for highway departments, landscape architects, garden clubs, plant nurseries, and other groups throughout the country who want to begin landscaping with native plants.

WILDFLOWER CENTER

There are many exciting things to see at the Wildflower Center:

- Young children enter the Little House through a tiny 3-ft door! Inside, they can learn about plants.
- Display gardens show how to landscape using native plants and flowers.
- A pollination garden shows how plants and animals interact.
- A sensory garden lets people experience the exotic smells and textures of some native plants. This garden is open to everyone, but it is specially designed for wheelchair users and for people who are visually impaired.
- A hummingbird garden, a songbird garden, and a deer-resistant garden show plants that attract hummingbirds and songbirds and plants that deer don't like!

Think & Do

Research plants that have different smells and textures. Sketch these plants in color. Then, using paper and colored pencils, plan your own sensory garden.

Fold

TEXAS LOOKS . . . LIKE TEXAS!

Each area's soil and climate make it the perfect environment for its own native plants. If people in each state used mostly native plants in landscaping, Texas would look like Texas, which would be very different from Florida. Every state would have a unique look of its own. Sometimes even within a state there can be many different geographic regions. Annual asters flourish in the pines and oaks near Tyler in the Gulf coastal plains of Texas, while the hill country around Austin, Texas, is home to bluebonnets (the Texas state flower), and Indian paintbrush.

In Your Own Backyard

Look at your own backyard. Are any native plants growing there, right under your nose? Here are some ways to find out about the wildflowers in your area:

- Visit a nursery that sells native plants, and ask to talk with the person who knows the most about them. Make a list of questions to ask before you go.
- Use your library, a bookstore, or the Internet to learn more about wildflowers native to your area.

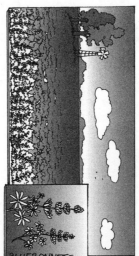

BLUEBONNETS

Indiana's Famous Dunes

Take-Home Book • 1

Fold

Harcourt

Science Fun

"Mom, Look What I Found!"

Some sands are rich in glacial mineral deposits called *placers*. Lake Michigan's sand contains a lot of quartz. But imagine the surprise of James Marshall, who found gold at Sutter's Mill in California in 1848. His discovery marked the beginning of the California gold rush.

LAKESHORE LAUGHS

▲ 1. What do mother sand crabs use to take their babies out for a stroll?

▲ 2. What's the standard lunch item at Indiana Dunes?

▲ 3. What did one sand hill say to the other?

Read More About Sand Dunes

Sand Dunes (a Carolrhoda Earth Watch book) by Jan Gumprecht Bannan

Sand on the Move: The Story of Dunes by Roy A. Gallant

I BET THE SURFING WAS GREAT IN THOSE DAYS!

Lake Michigan was this high in 8,000 B.C.

Answers to Vocabulary Fun: Across: 1. prickly pear, 3. savanna, 5. bearberry, 7. living, 9. marsh; Down: 2. Wisconsin, 4. Karner blue, 6. Mt. Baldy, 8. Michigan.

Answers to Science Fun: 1. dune buggies, 2. a sandwich, 3. Dune anything tonight?

WHAT'S SO SPECIAL ABOUT INDIANA DUNES?

Lots of things are special about Indiana Dunes. It's amazing that such a rich natural environment exists in the middle of an area filled with people and industry.

Indiana Dunes National Lakeshore is located on the southern banks of Lake Michigan and includes not only sand dunes but also a unique variety of plants, animals, and insects.

Indiana Dunes has the most diverse ecosystem in the entire Midwest. There are bird-filled marshes, oak and maple forests, and sand dunes. There is also an area of open oak savanna, one of the most endangered habitats in the entire world. The Midwest once had over 12 million hectares (about 30 million acres) of oak savanna. Now, 99.98 percent of the savanna no longer exists or is threatened.

VocabularyFun

Looking for Solid Ground

Complete the word puzzle with terms from the book.

ACROSS

1. A desert cactus that grows in the Indiana Dunes

3. About 30 million acres of oak that once existed in the Midwest

5. The Arctic plant that grows alongside 1 Across

7. A term for dunes that are constantly moving

9. One type of wetlands in the Indiana Dunes

DOWN

2. The glacier that helped form the Indiana Dunes

4. The endangered butterfly that lives in the Indiana Dunes

6. The most famous of the Indiana Dunes

8. The Great Lake out of which came much of the sand for the Indiana Dunes

Answers on page 8

FROM MOUNTAINS TO MOLEHILLS

Here's one way to see for yourself how erosion affects a sand dune.

MATERIALS

▲ sand
▲ container
▲ craft sticks
▲ watering can
▲ water

PROCEDURE

1. Build a small "sand dune" with friends. Place craft sticks at many different angles all over your dune to represent trees and plants.

2. Let a very gentle sprinkle of "rain" fall on the top of the mountain.

3. How does the water move down the sides of the dune?

4. What happened to the area around the sticks?

CONCLUSIONS

What could you do to decrease or stop the amount of sand moving down your dune? Brainstorm a list of ideas with your friends. Then rebuild your sand dune, and test your most promising ideas.

WALKING BACK IN TIME

As you start some distance away from the water's edge and walk slowly toward Lake Michigan, you pass the remains of what were once vast prairies. You move through forests, swamps, bogs, marshes, grasses, and, of course, the dunes. New environments were continually formed as the water level of the lake dropped over millions of years.

Building a Dune

These sand dunes are built by the winds from Lake Michigan. The winds lift the sand and carry it inland until plants and hills slow the wind enough that the weight of the sand drops it to the ground. Eventually, the sand begins to form into small mounds, which then slow more wind, causing more sand to drop. This process continues to build the mounds higher and higher into large dunes.

Mt. Baldy, the most famous dune at the park, is a "living" sand dune. It inches farther away from the lake a bit more each year. A hint about the reason it is moving is in Mt. Baldy's name. With no plants or trees to anchor it in place, the 40-m (about 135-ft) dune is constantly being cut down and built back up by the wind and water.

SLOW GROWTH

The environmental changes at Indiana Dunes didn't happen overnight. During the end of the Ice Age, massive blocks of ice swept across the continent. As the Wisconsin glacier advanced and retreated over the area that is now the Great Lakes region, it crushed everything underneath it, grinding rocks into pebbles and pebbles into sand.

Glacial Fallout

Because of the movement of glaciers, environments that normally would have never met suddenly came together at the Indiana Dunes. As a result, there are strange combinations of neighboring plants. For example, the Arctic bearberry grows next to a desert plant, the prickly pear.

Find Out

Where are the world's biggest sand dunes? How were they formed? Some sand dunes actually buried ancient towns for hundreds of years. Can you find out where these towns were?

FAST CHANGES IN EARTH'S SURFACE

Nature also has faster ways of changing the environment. Floods, volcanoes, and earthquakes all change the Earth's surface rapidly. Human activities can quickly change an environment, too. Long ago, periodic natural fires in the Indiana Dunes kept the area open and free of shade trees and shrubs. Now humans keep fires under control, and the open fields are slowly shrinking.

The open fields of the Indiana Dunes are home to the Karner blue butterfly. In fact, the Indiana Dunes has the third largest population in the world of Karner blues. This small, 1-in. butterfly once lived among

vast fields of wild lupine in open, sunny areas of the Indiana Dunes. Now the changes in the Indiana Dunes are destroying the Karner blue's natural habitat. These butterflies were put on the endangered-species list in 1972.

Think & Do

What environmental changes are taking place near where you live? Is a lake shrinking? Are trees or plants changing? Find examples, and illustrate or take photographs of a few.

RECYCLING COMPUTERS

FAST FACT

A 1991 study predicted that by the year 2005, there would be 150 million computers cluttering up landfills. In 1997 that prediction was reduced to 55 million.

FAST FACT

In 1998 the typical life span of a new computer in a work setting was two to three years.

TO: MAPLE ELEMENTARY
FROM: SOUTH HIGH SCHOOL

Fold

Harcourt

Science Fun

THE JOKE IS ON CPU

▶ 1. What does an environmentally friendly computer technician drive to work?

▶ 2. How did the lion break his computer?

▶ 3. What do you call someone who fixes old computer monitors?

Read More About Ecology and Recycling

Here are some fiction books you might enjoy.

• *Dinah for President* by Claudia Mills

• *The Trouble with Gramary* by Betty Levin

• *Earth to Matthew* by Paula Danziger

Answers to Vocabulary Fun: 1. circuit board, 2. diskette, 3. landfill, 4. computer jewelry, 5. plastic, 6. lead, 7. metal; Final Phrase: Recycle me.

Answers to Science Fun: 1. a motor re-cycle. 2. He took too many bytes out of it. 3. a screen saver.

THE ECOLOGY OF RECYCLING

Many people already recycle bottles, cans, aluminum, paper, and plastic bottles. Programs in many cities "rescue" restaurant food left over at the end of each day. This good food is packaged and distributed to people who do not have enough food to eat.

Why Recycle Old Computers?

- They take up a lot of room in landfills.
- Many of them are in good working order, or could be with a few repairs.
- They contain parts and materials that can be recycled separately.
- Computer monitors contain lead, which makes them dangerous to dump in landfills.

Find Out

What are the dangers of lead ending up in landfills? Present your findings in the form of a poster or write a letter to your local newspaper.

Fold

Vocabulary Fun

New Awareness for a New Day

Unscramble the vocabulary term in each box and write it on the line below the box. Use the letters in the circles to form a phrase.

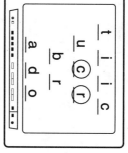

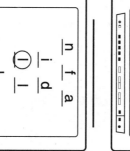

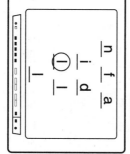

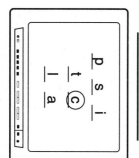

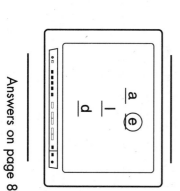

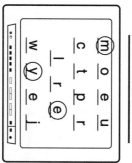

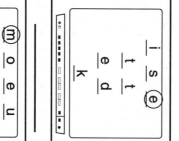

Answers on page 8

Harcourt

A RECYCLING STATE OF MIND

MATERIALS
▲ pencil and paper
▲ colored markers
▲ poster board

PROCEDURE

1. Review the parts of computers that can be recycled.

2. Challenge yourself to think of at least 5 to 10 uses for each one. Try to come up with a few ideas around which someone might start a business.

3. Now make a list of other mechanical items that are commonly thrown away.

CONCLUSIONS

What parts can be reclaimed and recycled? Can you combine items from the two lists? Put a star by your favorite ideas. Make a poster that lists them.

6 • Take-Home Book

Fold

RECYCLING 101

Suppose you are a business owner. You've just replaced every computer in your company with the latest and greatest model. The old computers are only two years old. What should you do with them?

A. Rent a trailer to take the old ones to the dump.

B. Keep them in a storage facility that charges several hundred dollars a month.

C. Find a company or group that takes old computers, repairs them if necessary, and finds good homes for them.

D. Donate the computers to a nonprofit organization that needs them.

If you picked D, you're not only thinking ecologically, you also made a smart business decision. Because you donated them to a nonprofit organization, your company gets a tax credit from the government.

Some high schools have started after-school programs that help interested students learn how to repair computers. The students earn a paycheck while they learn useful skills. The computers they repair are given to needy schools in their district, and the environment is saved from the harmful effects of dumping old computers.

Take-Home Book • 3

RECYCLING COMPUTER PARTS

What if computers can't be fixed? What can be recycled?

Hardware

▶ Chips and circuit boards: These are cleaned up and sold as clipboards, jewelry, and art pieces.

▶ Metal and plastic: All of the copper wire, steel and plastic cases, cables, and other metal and plastic pieces can be reclaimed, melted down, and reused.

Software

▶ Packaging: Almost all packaging can be recycled, including the box and even the shrinkwrap.

▶ Disks: A giant magnet removes the data, the labels are peeled off, and the disks are ready to reuse. Many software companies recycle their own disks or pay another company to duplicate new contents on the recycled disks for them.

▶ CDs: CDs can be ground up and melted down.

Fold

COMPUTERS AS ART

We know computers can be tools for drawing art. But what about computer parts as art? Like some artists, Portland, Oregon, artist Bonnie Meltzer uses her computer to help her design jewelry. Unlike most other artists, she makes her jewelry out of wire and recycled computer parts.

"The motor is very beautiful," she says, "with spokes wrapped with brightly colored wire. The [circuit] board looks like a tiny piece of southwest Native American art." She paints, sands, and cuts the parts she selects, joining them together to make her jewelry.

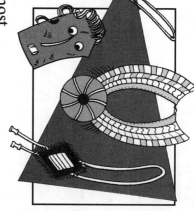

Think & Do

Ask a teacher, computer lab instructor, or a parent to let you look inside a computer. Study the circuit board. Think about what the parts could be used for. Then draw, paint, or color what your new piece of computer art will look like.

EL NIÑO MAKES A BIG IMPRESSION

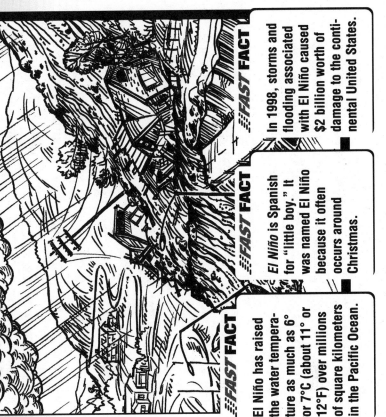

FAST FACT

El Niño has raised the water temperature as much as 6° or 7°C (about 11° or 12°F) over millions of square kilometers in the Pacific Ocean.

FAST FACT

El Niño is Spanish for "little boy." It was named El Niño because it often occurs around Christmas.

FAST FACT

In 1998, storms and flooding associated with El Niño caused $2 billion worth of damage to the continental United States.

Take-Home Book • 1

Harcourt

Science Fun

Surf's Up—Way, WAY Up

Big-wave surfers such as California resident Taylor Knox are used to riding waves 8 to 11 m (about 26 to 36 ft) high—the size of small apartment buildings. But El Niño took big-wave surfing to another level.

Knox traveled to Mexico's Todos Santos Islands, where, thanks to El Niño, he rode a wave more than 18 meters (about 60 ft) high! Scary? According to Knox, "It was like the best roller-coaster ride you could ever imagine!"

RIDDLES TO WEAR YOU DOWN!

▲ 1. How do fans of the Miami Hurricanes cheer their team on game day?

▲ 2. What is El Niño's favorite spot on the playground?

▲ 3. What did the storm cloud do when it was tired of raining cats and dogs?

Answers to Vocabulary Fun: El Niño: warm ocean waters, mild winters in the north, fewer hurricanes, fishing industry slackens; La Niña: cold ocean waters, cold winters in the north, many hurricanes, fishing industry booms.

Answers to Science Fun: 1. They do a tidal wave. 2. The mud-slide. 3. It hailed a taxi.

8 • Take-Home Book

WHAT IS EL NIÑO?

Once every seven to ten years, normal weather patterns are disrupted by periodic warming of the water in the Pacific Ocean. This weather pattern is called El Niño.

This weather pattern is called El Niño—short for El Niño southern oscillation. During El Niño, warm water from the equator pushes into the colder water found farther north. So far, scientists have not been able to predict when these conditions will occur or how severe they will be. When El Niño does strike, there is disruption in sea life, wildlife, and human life.

Usually, though not always, El Niño brings more rain than usual, and higher temperatures. The El Niño of 1997–1998, for example, was the strongest recorded this century. It increased snow packs in the mountains and caused warmer temperatures, weeks of relentless rain, hurricane-force winds, flooding, mudslides, massive crop failure, drought, and disease.

Fold

Vocabulary Fun

Use the descriptive words in the box below to fill in under the labels of El Niño and La Niña.

warm ocean waters   **fishing industry booms**
fewer hurricanes   **cold ocean waters**
many hurricanes   **fishing industry slackens**
mild winters in the north   **cold winters in the north**

El Niño   La Niña

Answers on page 8

Take-Home Book • 7

THE LONG ARM OF EL NIÑO

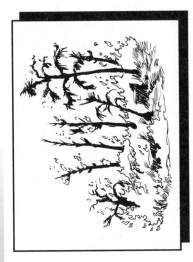

Although the El Niño currents are contained in the Pacific, their effects are felt worldwide. The 1997–1998 El Niño was particularly destructive.

In California, nearly 8000 sea lion pups died of starvation. The warming of the waters drove their natural food supply to cool, nutrient-rich waters farther north.

The 1997–1998 El Niño caused drought conditions in Australia and Florida, which led to severe crop failures and catastrophic fires.

El Niño's abnormally warm water temperatures created a condition known as coral bleaching in locations as far apart as Panama and the Indian Ocean. Coral bleaching is caused by the expulsion of a certain type of algae from the coral in reaction to the warmer water temperatures. The algae is essential to the coral's survival, and if the water temperature does not cool down quickly, the coral dies.

--- Fold ---

MAKE YOUR OWN BAROMETER

A barometer measures air pressure, which helps predict the weather.

MATERIALS

▲ scissors   ▲ small jar   ▲ straw   ▲ ruler

▲ balloon   ▲ rubber band   ▲ glue   ▲ clay

PROCEDURE

1. With the scissors, cut the neck from the balloon. Secure the balloon over the jar, using the rubber band.

2. With the scissors, cut the straw slantwise to make it pointed. With the pointed end sticking out, glue the other end to the balloon.

3. Set the ruler in clay so the ruler rises vertically. Place the ruler close enough to the straw to touch it, but not so close that the straw can't move. Record the number on the ruler to which the straw points.

4. Keep a record of the straw's positions. Record the weather for the day. Is there any relationship between the weather and the movement of the straw?

CONCLUSIONS

Your barometer measures air pressure. Low or falling air pressure indicates a storm is on the way. Then the barometer drops. On clear days the air pressure is high, so the barometer rises.

IS THERE ANY GOOD NEWS?

Not all of El Niño's effects are harmful. The increase in temperature means warmer-than-normal winters for many areas, which lowers energy usage and heating bills. Energy reports state that in 1998 the amount of energy used for heating dropped 10 percent. People in the United States usually spend $30 billion to heat their homes and $20 billion to heat workplaces. Ten percent of $50 billion is a saving of $5 billion in heating bills. And any fossil fuels not burned are conserved.

Likewise, the increase in precipitation that can accompany El Niño builds up the water table, helping cities where water levels are dangerously low. The increased water supply keeps the hydroelectric plants working full-time, producing more power and reducing costs.

El Niño also reduces the likelihood of severe hurricanes. It has been estimated that the 1997–1998 El Niño decreased hurricane damage in the United States by about $1 billion.

Pretend you're a small-business advisor. What would your top-ten small-business recommendations be for the next El Niño season?

WHAT TO DO ABOUT EL NIÑO

Following are some precautions we can take to help avoid the destruction caused by El Niño.

• Restore flood plains in areas prone to flooding.
• Reduce road-building, clear-cutting, and other erosion-promoting activities in areas at risk for mudslides.
• Increase tree-planting in those same areas.
• Toughen building codes in areas prone to damage from severe storms.

LA NIÑA

La Niña, or "little girl," is the cold twin of El Niño. La Niña usually, but not always, follows the warming trend of El Niño. La Niña causes the winter cold to arrive early and the temperatures to be lower than in the previous year. There are more summer thunderstorms, hurricanes, and heavy rains. La Niña brings colder winters to the Northeast and warmer temperatures to the Southeast.

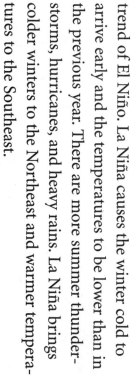

SUBMERSIBLES

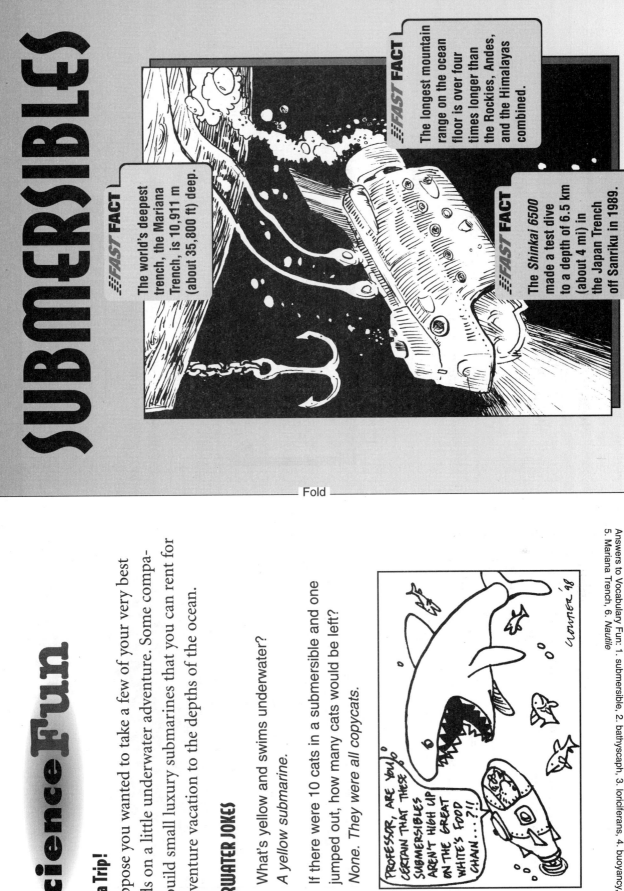

FAST FACT
The world's deepest trench, the Mariana Trench, is 10,911 m (about 35,800 ft) deep.

FAST FACT
The longest mountain range on the ocean floor is over four times longer than the Rockies, Andes, and the Himalayas combined.

FAST FACT
The *Shinkai 6500* made a test dive to a depth of 6.5 km (about 4 mi) in the Japan Trench off Sanriku in 1989.

Fold

Harcourt

Science Fun

What a Trip!

Suppose you wanted to take a few of your very best friends on a little underwater adventure. Some companies build small luxury submarines that you can rent for an adventure vacation to the depths of the ocean.

UNDERWATER JOKES

▲ Q: What's yellow and swims underwater?
  A: *A yellow submarine.*

▲ Q: If there were 10 cats in a submersible and one jumped out, how many cats would be left?
  A: *None. They were all copycats.*

PROFESSOR, ARE YOU CERTAIN THAT THESE SUBMERSIBLES AREN'T HIGH UP ON THE GREAT WHITE'S FOOD CHAIN...?!!

Cronier '98

Answers to Vocabulary Fun: 1. submersible, 2. bathyscaph, 3. loriciferans, 4. buoyancy, 5. Mariana Trench, 6. *Nautile*

Some people prefer to work in offices, schools, or stores. Other people love to work outside. Still others like to travel. Being an oceanographer combines a bit of all of these environments.

Suppose you work in a small, round chamber big enough for three people. Safely enclosed in your "bubble," you are an adventurer, exploring the unknown. But you are not going *up* in space or *across* a desert or the white Arctic tundra. Your wilderness is *down* into the depths of the ocean.

This would not be possible without the invention of small research submarines, or submersibles. Auguste Piccard made a major breakthrough in the 1940s with the invention of the bathyscaph (BATH•i•skaf). A bathyscaph is a crewed, navigable submersible. Then in 1960 Piccard's son used a bathyscaph to dive into the Mariana Trench, the lowest known place on Earth.

Fold

VocabularyFun

Mixed-Up Words

Unscramble the letters to find some words used in this book about exploring the deep ocean. Use the circled letters to form the word that answers Question 6.

1. SLUMIBESERB ___ ___ ___ ___ ___ ⃝ ___ ___ ⃝ ___
2. THAPYBSCHA ___ ___ ___ ___ ___ ⃝ ___ ___ ___ ___
3. SCOILFIRRANE ___ ___ ___ ___ ___ ___ ___ ___ ___ ___ ⃝
4. YYACUNOB ___ ___ ___ ⃝ ___ ___ ___ ___
5. NIMAARA ___ ⃝ ___ ___ ___ ___ ___
   NERTCH ___ ___ ___ ___ ___ ___
6. What is the name of the submersible that explored the wreck of the *Titanic* deep under the ocean?

   the ___ ___ ___ ___ ___ ___

Answers on page 8

THE MYSTERIOUS OCEAN

The ocean has been a mystery to people in many cultures throughout the ages. Along with outer space, it is an environment that holds many secrets. Right now, we have better maps of the moon and Venus than we have of the deep ocean. Oceanographers in the next century may change that.

Why has it been so difficult to study the deep ocean? For one thing, the ocean is not a friendly environment for humans. It is dark and very cold. Deep water exerts extremely high pressure that can be fatal. Submersibles provide the air, warmth, and light humans need. And they are built of strong materials that resist the pressure exerted by the water.

The submersible *Nautile* explored the 3800-m (about 12,467-ft) deep wreck of the *Titanic*. The lights of the submersible allowed the men inside to view up to 15 m (about 50 ft) around them. As the *Nautile* glided in and around the sunken ship, its two arms were used to recover artifacts. The men made a videotape and took photographs of the area. Researchers were then able to learn more about why and how the ship sank.

— Fold —

THE ORANGE SUBMERSIBLE

For a submersible to dive, air must be released from the ballast. This allows the craft to sink freely.

MATERIALS

▲ fresh orange peel
▲ butter knife
▲ ballpoint pen
▲ bottle with a plastic lid

PROCEDURE

1. Cut a small piece out of the fresh orange peel, and use it for a submersible.
2. Make portholes on your submersible with a ballpoint pen.
3. Fill the bottle to the top with water.
4. Place the submersible in the bottle.
5. Close the bottle with a plastic cap.
6. Now press on the cap with your finger. What happens?
7. Release the lid. What happens to the submersible?

CONCLUSIONS

The orange-peel submersible floats because it contains tiny air bubbles. Why does the submersible sink when you press down on the cap? (The bubbles are pushed out of the orange by pressure—from your finger—that passes through the water to the orange peel. This decreases the peel's buoyancy and makes it go down.)

SUBMERSIBLE REQUIREMENTS

A submersible needs to be able to sink, to rise, and to float underwater. It does this by adjusting its weight with tanks that can be filled with either air or water. Water increases the weight, sending the submersible into deeper water. Air decreases the weight, allowing the craft to rise.

Submersibles are designed to do delicate underwater tasks at great depths. Sometimes they are guided by remote controls from a support ship. A person on the ship controls mechanical arms as they explore the ocean floor and collect samples. At other times, submersibles carry people who, in their safe underwater environment, conduct experiments and observe the ocean firsthand.

Harcourt

— Fold —

Surprising Discoveries

Using submersibles, scientists have found deep pockets of water at the bottom of the Red Sea that are extremely hot and salty. It is thought that this water seeps from rocks under the surface and doesn't mix with the water above it.

In 1986, biologists discovered a brand-new major group of animals called *loriciferans* (lawr•ih•SIF•er•anz). These microscopic creatures live in mud between grains of sand.

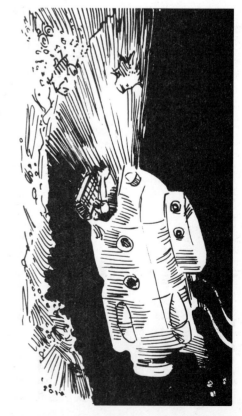

Think & Do

What if you are designing the first underwater living space? What would this underwater home look like? What features would it need to have? What features would you add for fun?

CLOSE ENCOUNTERS

Mapping the Moon

Harcourt

Science Fun

Moon Is Made of Swiss Cheese

Some people used to think the moon was made of cheese. The Egyptians believed the moon was the god Osiris, who died and came back to life each month. In a German tale, the Old-Man-in-the-Moon was a villager who had been caught stealing cabbages. As a punishment, he was placed on the moon as a warning to others.

How many nursery rhymes and myths can you find that seek to explain this mysterious ball in the sky? After reading some of these myths, make up and illustrate a moon myth of your own.

SPACE-AGE RIDDLES

▲ 1. Why couldn't the astronauts land on the moon?

▲ 2. Why did the teacups board the spaceship?

▲ 3. Why did the cow jump over the moon?

Answers to Vocabulary Fun: 1. orbit; 2. rotate, axis; 3. telescope; 4. satellite, revolve; 5. space probe

Answers to Science Fun: 1. It was full. 2. to search for flying saucers. 3. She needed more space.

EARLY MAPS

The first known map of the moon was drawn about 1600 by William Gilbert, the physician to Queen Elizabeth I. The telescope had not yet been invented. He simply gazed up at the sky and drew what he saw. The invention of the telescope a few years later made it possible to see many more features on the moon.

In 1647 Johannes Hevelius built an observatory on the roof of his house, using the best instruments available at the time. Hevelius was one of the leading 17th century observational astronomers. He named the lunar features he saw and added the names to his map. Copies of Hevelius's map still exist, but the original copper printing plate no longer does. After his death, it was apparently melted down and made into a teapot.

Photo Maps

In the late 1800s and early 1900s, photographic atlases of the moon began to appear. Since that time, lunar mapping has been done photographically. When it became possible to reach the moon with rockets, accurate maps were more than interesting. They were necessary to astronauts landing on the moon.

Vocabulary Fun

Phone call from the space shuttle! Great, but it's in code. The code corresponds to a touch-tone telephone pad. Each number has three letters represented by a /, |, and \. Can you break the code to fill in the missing words in each sentence? Ex.

A B C
/ | \   [2]

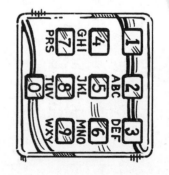

1. John Glenn was the first astronaut to 6 7 2 4 8 the Earth in 1968.
/ | \ | / \

2. What if you saw the Earth 7 6 8 2 8 3 on its 2 9 4 7?
___ ___
/ | \ | / \

3. John Glenn did not need a 8 3 5 3 7 2 6 7 3 to view the Earth from space.
___
| / \   / | \

4. On his second trip into space in 1998, Glenn was able to view a 7 2 8 3 5 5 4 8 3 7 3 8 6 5 8 3 around the Earth.
___ ___
/ | \ | / \   / | \ | / \

5. Glenn was able to investigate a 7 7 2 2 3 7 7 6 2 3.
___ ___
\ | \   / | \   / | \ | | |

Harcour

MOON MAPS

Even though we may know more scientific information about the moon than early people did, it is still possible to feel the wonder they felt looking up at this mysterious, ever-changing, bright object in the sky.

MATERIALS

▲ large sheets of paper ▲ masking tape ▲ eraser
▲ drawing board ▲ drawing pencils

PROCEDURE

1. Go outside on the next clear, dry night when there is a full moon. Take some time to look at it.

2. Place your paper on the drawing board, and tape it down at the corners.

3. Draw the shape of the moon so that it takes up most of your paper. Then use your eyes to draw the moon's surface in as much detail as you can.

CONCLUSIONS

Where are the darkest places? What places are lightest? Do you see shapes? Take your time to make your drawing of the moon as detailed as possible. Look through a pair of binoculars. What do you see now? Can you add some details to your drawing?

LUNAR LANDSCAPES

The moon is truly an alien landscape. Two main types of terrain have been identified:

- heavily cratered and very old highlands
- relatively smooth and younger maria

Before robotic and piloted spacecraft went to the moon, most scientists thought that lunar craters were volcanic. Now they think differently.

Impact Theory

Moon rocks and sediment brought back by the *Apollo 11* astronauts have led to a new theory about how the moon and the Earth formed. This *impact theory* maintains that Earth probably collided with a very large object (as big as Mars, or bigger) and that the moon formed from the material ejected from Earth by the impact. Scientists hope to test this theory further by collecting samples from different places on the moon.

CLEMENTINE DISCOVERIES

In the summer of 1994, the moon was extensively mapped by the spacecraft *Clementine*. Data from *Clementine* suggests that there may be water ice in some deep craters near the moon's south pole. There may be ice at the north pole as well.

The Earth's active geology, including volcanic activity and erosion, has erased much of the evidence of geologic processes that have shaped Earth. On the moon the evidence is still intact. Scientists have long wondered what happened to the dinosaurs on Earth. Scientists have gathered information by studying the moon's many craters formed during the 600 million years for which we have rich fossil records on Earth. They now suspect that a gigantic impact event on Earth may have caused the dinosaurs' extinction.

Think & Do

The gravity on the moon's surface is about one-sixth of the gravity on Earth. If you could leap 1.5 m (about 5 ft) on Earth, how many meters could you leap if you were on the moon? Measure to see how high that would be.

LIVING ON THE MOON

Suppose you were among the first adventurers to start a moon settlement. There would be a lot to do.

• Geologists would study the moon up close, with an emphasis on field trips.

• Writers, artists, and musicians would be inspired by the new landscape.

• Mining and chemical engineers would learn how to use the moon's resources.

• Life scientists would learn how to grow plants in solar greenhouses.

What other people would you include? Explain.

Rock Art

Twenty years after the landing of *Apollo 11*, scientists are still studying the samples brought back from that mission. Most of the *Apollo 11* treasures are stored at the Lunar Curatorial Facility (LCF) at the Johnson Space Center in Houston, Texas.

Find Out

The first piece of an interplanetary space station was launched from Russia in November 1998. What is the purpose of this exciting global venture? What problems must be solved to make it happen?

AURORA BOREALIS/ AURORA AUSTRALIS

FAST FACT
Some auroras are so bright that people can read by their light!

FAST FACT
Auroras are thought to occur in the atmospheres of other planets, such as Venus.

FAST FACT
The powerful solar storms that cause auroras confuse some animals. For example, homing pigeons that are released have a hard time finding their way home.

Fold

Harcourt

Science Fun

A Cool Place to Stay

The best places to see auroras are far north in the Northern Hemisphere. Tourists who visit Jukkasjarvi, Sweden, can see the aurora borealis and *also* test their endurance of very cold weather by reserving a room in the Ice Hotel! Each year, 4000 tons of ice are used

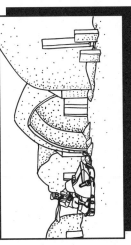

to make a 14-room hotel. Upon arrival, you'll get a thermal jumpsuit to help you withstand below-freezing temperatures. Your bed is a block of ice covered with a reindeer skin. For your sleeping comfort, you'll receive an insulated body bag like the kind that astronauts use. The hotel is open each year—until it begins to melt during an aurora!

Aurora Limerick

I went to the Jukkasjarvi palace
To see the aurora australis.
The man at the gate
Said "I'm sorry, my mate—
The one we've got's borealis."

FIRE IN THE SKY

An aurora is a natural display of light in the night sky that can be seen only in the far northern and southern regions of Earth. Auroras center on the Earth's magnetic poles. In the Northern Hemisphere, this often-colorful light display is called the Northern Lights, or the *aurora borealis* (aw•RAWR•uh bawr•ee•AL•is). In the Southern Hemisphere, it is called the *aurora australis* (aw•RAWR•uh aw•STRAY•lis).

The Power of the Sun

Auroras are caused by electrons and protons released by the sun as solar wind. After it leaves the sun, solar wind takes about two days to reach Earth. The particles are caught in Earth's magnetic field, which pulls the particles toward Earth's magnetic poles and pushes them down into the atmosphere. As the electrons and protons hit the gases in Earth's atmosphere, they cause the gases to glow. These glowing gases are the auroras that we see. Most auroras occur from about 90 to 130 km (55 to 80 mi) above Earth. The highest one ever measured was about 1100 km (about 700 mi) above Earth. They can extend across the sky for thousands of kilometers.

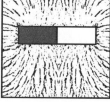

Fold

Vocabulary Fun

Awesome Auroras

Unscramble the letters, and answer the following riddles to learn the origin of some of the words in this book.

1. I am named after the Roman goddess of the dawn. RAAROU _____

2. My name comes from a kind of stone found in the ancient city of Magnesia. TANGEM _____

3. I got my name from Boreas, the Greek god of the north wind. ABOISREL _____

4. My name comes from the Latin word for "south wind." SAURSITAL _____

5. I was named after the ancient Greek word for "amber" because rubbing amber with a cloth produces a charge. TELONCER _____

A NEW APPROACH

For a long time, scientists thought auroras occurred most frequently during peak periods in an 11-year solar cycle. New research shows that this is not true. Auroras are now thought to be more or less constant. They are sometimes compared with another discharge process—lightning.

Observing Auroras

There is much to be learned about auroras. The study of auroras is an exciting focus for many scientists. They are now able to observe auroras using radar and a new instrument called an "all-sky camera." Scientists also can cause auroras to occur in laboratories and in space in order to study them.

Aurora Power

It takes 1000 billion watts of power to cause a typical aurora. Some scientists are thinking about ways to harness this power. If this happens, auroras will do more than light up the sky. They may also help light up homes and offices.

Take-Home Book • 3

— Fold —

FIELD TESTING

A magnetic field is the direction and amount of force that can be felt near a magnet.

MATERIALS

▶ gloves ▶ paper cup ▶ steel wool ▶ sheet of paper
▶ goggles ▶ scissors ▶ 2 magnets ▶ pin

PROCEDURE

1. Put on your gloves and goggles. Set the paper cup in front of you. Use scissors to cut the steel wool into tiny pieces and let the pieces fall into the cup.

2. Lay one magnet down, and cover it with the paper.

3. Gently tap some of the steel wool from the cup onto the paper covering the magnet.

4. Gently tap the paper. What happens to the steel wool? What kind of pattern is produced? Make a sketch of it.

5. Bring the pin toward the magnet. When do you feel the pull?

6. Try the experiment again using two magnets with opposite poles about 1 to 2 in. apart. Place the paper over both magnets, sprinkle on the steel wool, and tap gently. What happens?

CONCLUSIONS

How does this experiment help your understanding of auroras?

6 • Take-Home Book

Flashes, Arcs, and Bands

Auroras come in many shapes, sizes, and colors. One thing is for certain. Auroras do not bore the observer!

Some auroras glow, while others flash. Some appear as pulsating arcs through the sky. Auroras sometimes look like small spots or patches, while others resemble flaming bands of light fanning rapidly upward. Some auroras look like giant draperies hung in the sky.

Auroras appear in many colors. Green is most common, but deep red, bright pink, yellow, blue, violet, and purple are also seen.

Find Out

Research to find out what gases are struck by the electrons in the solar winds that spiral down near Earth. Make a chart that shows which gases cause certain colors. Which colors are rarely seen in auroras, and why? How does the distance of the gases from Earth affect the colors seen in an aurora?

Fold

Swirls of Inspiration

Auroras have awed people from different cultures for thousands of years. Historians believe that the idea of fire-breathing dragons came from the swaying motions and colors of auroras.

In Viking lore of ancient Finland, red auroras were called "fox fire," after the glistening fur of red foxes shimmering against the mountains. Some Inuit peoples in northern Alaska believed the lights were alive and would harm you if you whistled at them. Children were warned not to whistle at the lights.

"Talking" Lights

Some people have described crackling, swishing, and tinkling sounds accompanying some auroras. This may be true, but scientists have not yet proven that auroras make sounds.

Think & Do

Make up a myth of your own to explain what auroras are or where they come from. Turn your story into a picture book. Share your finished story with younger children.

H₂O SPORTS

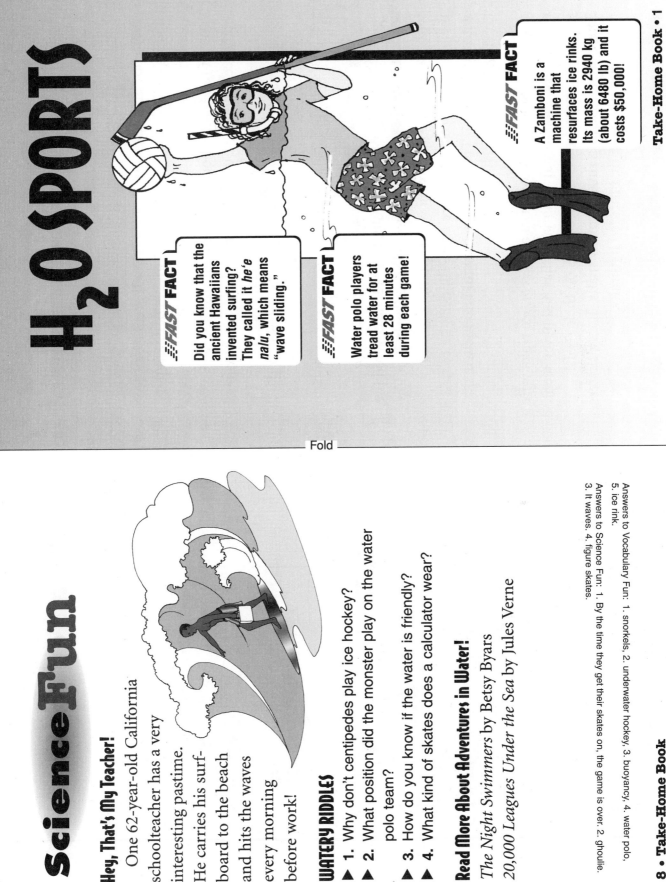

FAST FACT
Did you know that the ancient Hawaiians invented surfing? They called it *he'e nalu*, which means "wave sliding."

FAST FACT
Water polo players tread water for at least 28 minutes during each game!

FAST FACT
A Zamboni is a machine that resurfaces ice rinks. Its mass is 2940 kg (about 6480 lb) and it costs $50,000!

Fold

Science Fun

Hey, That's My Teacher!

One 62-year-old California schoolteacher has a very interesting pastime. He carries his surfboard to the beach and hits the waves every morning before work!

WATERY RIDDLES

▲ 1. Why don't centipedes play ice hockey?
▲ 2. What position did the monster play on the water polo team?
▲ 3. How do you know if the water is friendly?
▲ 4. What kind of skates does a calculator wear?

Read More About Adventures in Water!

The Night Swimmers by Betsy Byars
20,000 Leagues Under the Sea by Jules Verne

Answers to Vocabulary Fun: 1. snorkels, 2. underwater hockey, 3. buoyancy, 4. water polo, 5. ice rink.
Answers to Science Fun: 1. By the time they get their skates on, the game is over. 2. ghoulie. 3. It waves. 4. figure skates.

Harcourt

ICE SPORTS

In your grandparents' or great-grandparents' day, ice-skating could be enjoyed only outdoors in very cold weather on a natural body of water covered by a thick layer of ice. If somebody hadn't discovered a way to make ice indoors, you wouldn't be able to watch your

favorite figure skaters on TV or meet your friends at the local rink.

Henry Kirk knew that evaporation produces intense cold. In 1842, he covered the floor of his cellar in London with ice he made by mixing water, alum, salts, and melted sulfur. To make the ice more slippery, he coated it with hog's grease. The ice smelled awful and melted quickly.

By 1904, after a lot more trial and error, ice rinks were everywhere, even in warm climates that had never seen ice before. Fancy hotels had ice rinks on their roofs! There are ice-skating rinks in many malls. Today, skaters rarely set foot on ice that formed naturally.

Vocabulary Fun

Surf's Up

Help each surfer unscramble the letters in his or her fish, and write the word on the surfboard.

1. something that sticks out of the mouths of underwater hockey players

2. invented by British scuba divers in the 1950s

4. similar to soccer, but played in water

5. special footwear needed to go here

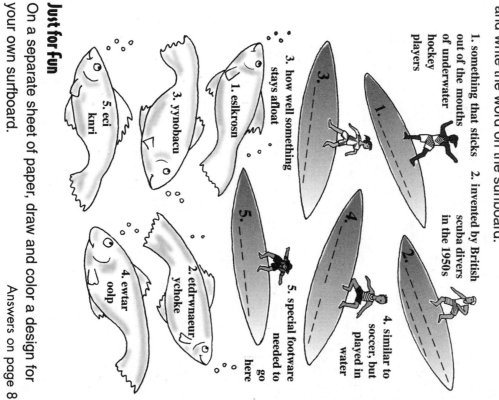

Just for Fun

On a separate sheet of paper, draw and color a design for your own surfboard.

1. eslkrosn

3. yynobacu

5. eci knri

3. how well something stays afloat

2. etdrwnaeur ychoke

4. ewtar oolp

Answers on page 8

Harcourt

WATER POLO

Water polo is sort of like hockey, but it's played without sticks. It's a little like soccer, except you use your hands instead of your feet. It's somewhat like basketball, but there are six players instead of five. And water polo is different from all these games because it's played in the water.

Water polo players have to tread water for the entire game. This means they can't touch the bottom or the sides of the pool. Also, they can only touch the ball with one hand. The object of the game is to carry the ball to the opponent's side.

Water polo started in England in the early 1800s and was played in rivers and lakes. Water polo is a form of rugby football, which is like soccer in the United States. Water polo quickly became popular and was one of the first team sports introduced in the 1900 Paris Olympics.

Think & Do

Make up your own water sport! Think about how playing a sport or game you know would be different if you played it in the water. How would the rules need to be changed? Write down some rules and regulations for your new game.

— Fold —

Harcourt

WAVE ACTION

Try this experiment outside, so you don't make any waves with your parents.

MATERIALS

▲ a discarded fish tank ▲ fine sand ▲ food coloring
▲ plastic disks, such as checkers, from a board game

PROCEDURE

1. Fill your fish tank about $\frac{3}{4}$ full of water. Add about 0.5 cm (0.25 in.) fine sand to the tank.

2. Lift one end of the tank and watch the water move. When the wave sloshes against the other end of the tank, lower your end and watch it move back. Do this for a while, until you feel the rhythm of the *ripple waves*.

3. What patterns are made in the sand with these waves? What happens when the wave moves back in the other direction?

4. How can you make the wave action easier to see? Place some of the plastic disks on the bottom. Watch what happens while a friend lifts the tank for you.

CONCLUSIONS

Water in motion has a lot of energy. What did you feel when the water was moving inside the tank? What do you think it would take to stop a wave once it starts?

ANCIENT BEACH BOYS

When you think of surfing, you probably imagine shirts with palm trees on them and the Beach Boys singing in the background. But did you know that surfing has been around since the 1500s? Early carvings in caves on the big island of Hawai'i show pictures of some of the first surfers.

Surfing in ancient Hawai'i was a religious practice perfected by the kings, queens, and high chiefs. They had a lot of time to practice and to perfect this difficult sport.

Ancient Hawaiians surfed on large wooden boards. Later, surfboards were designed to make them more aerodynamic. In the 1950s, Robert Wilson Simmons introduced balsa wood into surfboards. This light, spongy material made surfboards more buoyant, so they floated more easily until surfers caught a wave.

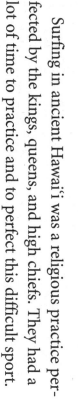

Find Out

Ancient Hawaiians surfed on boards that were 5.5 m (about 18 ft) long. The boards used today are different in both length and shape. Find out the length of the *shortboard* and the *longboard*. Why do you think the length has changed?

Fold

PLAY HOCKEY WHERE?

Underwater, of course! Underwater hockey, a game invented by British scuba divers in the 1950s, is now officially recognized by the U.S. Olympic Committee.

Underwater hockey players, six to a team, wear masks, snorkels, and fins. They don't rely on any supplemental oxygen. They take a deep breath and then go underwater for 15 to 30 seconds to make a play. Stick in hand, they try to move the puck across the pool floor into their opponent's goal.

The pool floor is slippery to reduce injury and to help the puck glide easily. A good flick sends a puck flying more than 4.5 m (about 15 ft) across and almost 50 cm (about 20 in.) above the pool bottom! How do you suppose someone coaches, watches, and officiates at underwater hockey games?

Windsurfing

One of the country's top windsurfing spots is in the Columbia River Gorge near Hood River, Oregon. Windsurfers use their own energy and specially designed boards to leap and sail over the waves. They learn to read the waves and the wind, so they can predict the amount of force needed to control their boards.

Harcourt

Science Fun

Don't Be a Fool!

Iron pyrite is a mineral that looks so much like gold it's called fool's gold. You've just been handed something that looks like gold, but you're no fool. You want to make sure it's really gold. How can you tell? Simple. You can:

- weigh it. (Fool's gold is less dense than real gold.)
- drop acid on it. (Fool's gold will dissolve.)
- drag it across a white tile. (Fool's gold leaves a black mark. Real gold doesn't.)

Awesome Fireworks

Did you know that metal compounds are responsible for the colorful fireworks you see on July 4th?

lead—blue   sodium compound—orange
copper—blue-green   lithium—red
potassium—lilac   barium—brown-green

RUSTY RIDDLES

▲ 1. Why did the gold miner wait ten years after gold was discovered to move to California?

▲ 2. What kind of music do steel workers prefer?

▲ 3. What metal directs traffic?

▲ 4. What is green and orange?

Answers to Vocabulary Fun: 1. malleable, 2. coke, 3. electron-sea model, 4. ductile, 5. hematite, 6. Iron Age, 7. Bronze Age; magnesium.

Answers to Science Fun: 1. He wanted to avoid the rush. 2. heavy metal. 3. cop-per. 4. a rusty pickle.

8 • Take-Home Book

METALS
Which One to Choose?

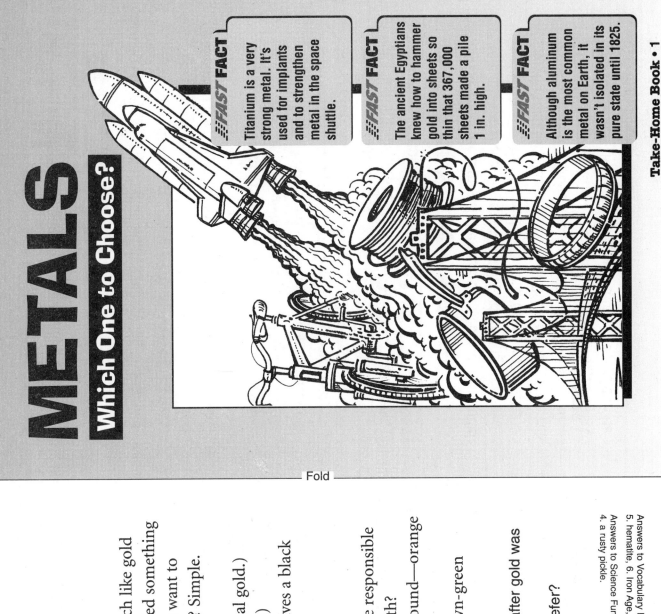

FAST FACT Titanium is a very strong metal. It's used for implants and to strengthen metal in the space shuttle.

FAST FACT The ancient Egyptians knew how to hammer gold into sheets so thin that 367,000 sheets made a pile 1 in. high.

FAST FACT Although aluminum is the most common metal on Earth, it wasn't isolated in its pure state until 1825.

METAL BASICS

Most metals, like pure gold, are shiny and can reflect light. Most metals are strong, hard, and have high melting points. Some are good conductors of electricity and thermal energy, and some, such as iron and nickel, are magnetic. Metals are malleable, which means they can be hammered into thin sheets. They are also ductile, which means they can be drawn out into thin wires. One ounce of gold can be heated and stretched to make a wire 100 km (about 60 mi) long! Hard metals ring when they're hit. Most metals are very reactive. They lose their electrons easily to form compounds with nonmetallic elements.

A Sea of Electrons

Scientists use a model they call the electron-sea model to explain the properties of metals. According to this model, in a piece of metal the nuclei of the atoms are surrounded by a sea of electrons. These electrons act as a kind of glue that holds the metal together. Because the electrons are able to move around so easily, they conduct electricity and thermal energy and allow the metal to be deformed easily.

2 • Take-Home Book

Fold

VocabularyFun

Use the definitions to help you unscramble the words. Then use the circled letters to form the word that finishes the sentence that follows.

1. LLMEELBAA ○ __ __ __ __ __ __ __ able to be hammered into thin sheets

2. EKOC __ __ ○ __ a kind of coal used in extracting iron from iron ore

3. NOCTRELE-AES LODEM __ __ __ __ __ __ __ - __ __ __ ○ __ __ __ __ a model for describing the arrangement of atoms and electrons in metals

4. CILUDET __ ○ __ __ __ ○ __ able to be drawn out into thin wires

5. EITHAMET __ __ __ __ ○ __ __ __ a mineral containing iron combined with oxygen

6. NORI GEA __ __ __ __ __ ○ __ the time we presently live in, named after the metal from which we make most tools and weapons

7. ZEBRON EAG __ __ __ __ ○ __ __ __ __ the time during which most tools and weapons were made of a mixture of copper and tin

What important metal is lighter than aluminum and is extracted from sea water? __ __ __ __ __ __ __ __ __

Answers on page 8

Take-Home Book • 7

TH62   Unit E • Chapter 2

METALS IN MINERALS

If you go for a walk in the country, metal atoms are in the rocks all around you. But you won't find much metal you can recognize. This is because most metals are too reactive to occur in nature in their pure state. In Earth's crust most metals are combined with other elements such as sulfur, oxygen, and silicon to form minerals.

Hematite, magnetite, and limonite contain large amounts of iron. To use the iron in these minerals, you have to get rid of the oxygen in them. In the United States, this is done mostly in blast furnaces. In a blast furnace, iron ore, limestone, and coke (a form of coal) are heated with a blast of air at 760°C to 1150°C (1400°F to about 2100°F). The hot air burns the coke to form carbon monoxide gas, which reacts with the iron ore and removes the oxygen. In the process, the temperature in the furnace goes up to 1600°C (about 3000°F), melting the iron.

Find Out

Find out what aluminum ore is and how people extract aluminum metal from it. Why do you think it took so long for people to figure out how to extract aluminum?

Fold

OBSERVE A METAL REACT

MATERIALS

▲ thermometer
▲ jar with lid
▲ steel wool pad
▲ vinegar

PROCEDURE

1. Place the thermometer in the jar and close the lid. Wait five minutes and record the temperature.

2. Remove the thermometer from the jar. Wrap the steel wool pad around the bulb of the thermometer. Place them into the jar and close the lid. Wait five minutes and record the temperature.

3. Remove the thermometer and the steel wool pad from the jar. Soak half the steel wool pad in vinegar for one minute. Squeeze excess vinegar out of the steel wool, and wrap it around the bulb of the thermometer. Place the thermometer and the steel wool into the jar and close the lid. Wait five minutes. Record your observations.

CONCLUSIONS

After the steel wool was soaked in vinegar, the temperature rose. This is because the vinegar removed the protective coating from the steel wool, allowing the iron in the steel to combine with oxygen in the air and form rust. The reaction of iron with oxygen releases thermal energy, which made the temperature rise.

METALS USED IN THE PAST

Copper is less reactive than most other metals. It can occur in nature as a pure metal, uncombined with other elements. Copper is also malleable, or soft. For this reason copper was one of the first metals found and used by humans.

Around 3500 B.C., people learned they could make copper harder by melting it with arsenic. The resulting mixture was called bronze. By 3000 B.C., people had replaced the arsenic in bronze with tin. This period was called the Bronze Age, because people made tools and weapons out of bronze.

Around 1500 B.C., methods were developed for working with iron. Earth's crust contains much more iron ore than copper. So once people knew how to use iron, tools and weapons made from this metal became common. This period of history is called the Iron Age. We are still in the Iron Age.

Like copper, gold and silver are less reactive than most other metals. They can be found in Earth's crust as pure metals. Gold was used for ornaments, jewelry, and cooking utensils as early as 3500 B.C. Silver was used from about 2400 B.C.

METALS USED TODAY

Aluminum Aluminum is used by many manufacturers because of its light weight, strength, and the ease with which it can be shaped. The auto industry is replacing some of the steel in cars with aluminum to decrease their weight and increase their fuel efficiency.

Zinc Zinc is the fourth most used metal in the world. It is used primarily as a coating on steel to prevent corrosion.

Platinum Platinum is mostly associated with jewelry, but it has a home in industry, too. Platinum is used to make cleaner diesel fuel and engine oil. It is also used in nitrogen fertilizers for farming.

Plutonium Most well-known as a raw material for making nuclear bombs, plutonium is also used as a heat source for components on outer space probes. To keep the probe operating, radiated energy from the plutonium is converted to electrical energy.

Think & Do

Look at the Periodic Table to find a metal that has not been discussed here. Find out where it comes from and how it is used.

Harcourt

THE SCIENCE OF OLYMPIC AND OTHER SPORTS

FAST FACT

To change the direction of a baseball that's going 145 km/hr (about 90 mi/hr), the bat must push on it with 35,600 Newtons (about 8000 lb) of force.

FAST FACT

Some basketball players jump almost 1 m (about 3 ft) into the air when going up for a slam dunk.

FAST FACT

Today, sprinters run the 100-m (about 330-ft) dash in less than 10 seconds, at least 2 seconds faster than the world record in 1897.

Harcourt

Science Fun

Olympic Gold

In 1904, Olympic gymnastics history was made. George Eyser of the United States won five medals, including two gold. What made his performance so remarkable? Eyser had a wooden leg!

Tara Lipinski made her debut in world figure skating at the age of 13. In 1997, Tara returned to win the World Championship at the age of 14. She was the youngest athlete ever to win. Tara won a gold medal at the 1998 winter Olympics as the youngest competitor.

SPORTS RIDDLES

▲ 1. What does the baseball coach say when the cake is done?

▲ 2. Why did the ice skater bring his skates to the birthday party?

▲ 3. What is used by basketball players and people who embroider?

▲ 4. What basketball skill do babies excel at?

▲ 5. Why did the athletes laugh at Cinderella?

Answers to Vocabulary Fun: 1. baseball, 2. sprinter, 3. slam-dunk 4. accelerate, 5. curve ball, 6. luge, 7. blades, 8. friction, 9. feet, Clue word: chariot.

Answers to Science Fun: 1. Batter up! 2. He heard there was icing on the cake. 3. hoops. 4. dribbling. 5. She had a pumpkin for a coach.

SPORTS AND SCIENCE

Life in the Olympic Fast Lane

Olympic speed skaters look as though they're gliding effortlessly over the ice. But in reality, it's not that easy. Our natural urge when we walk or run is to push down and backward with our feet in order to accelerate. Speed skaters learn to keep their blades level and to push out to the side to accelerate.

Pllllaaaayyyy Ball!

Have you ever wondered what makes a curve ball curvy? A curve ball spins so that the top of the ball moves back toward the pitcher while the bottom of the ball moves away from the pitcher. Because of the spin, the top of the ball moves in the same direction as the air, while the bottom moves against the air. This means that the velocity of the air is greater on the bottom of the ball. There is also more stress on the air at the bottom of the ball, making it *break away* from the ball's surface sooner, while the air at the top *hangs onto* it. These forces give the ball a lift that curves it toward third base.

VocabularyFun

Get These Balls in Order!

Each of these contains a term that has to do with the Olympics and other sports. Use the clues to help you write the word in the spaces provided.

1. ⎯ ⎯ ◯ ⎯ ⎯ ⎯ ⎯ ⎯ a game played in the summer

2. ⎯ ◯ ⎯ ⎯ ⎯ ⎯ ⎯ ⎯ one who runs fast for a short time

3. ⎯ ⎯ ⎯ ⎯ - ⎯ ⎯ ⎯ Michael Jordan could do this

4. ⎯ ⎯ ◯ ⎯ ⎯ ⎯ ⎯ to speed up

5. ⎯ ⎯ ◯ ⎯ ⎯ ⎯ tricky to hit

6. ⎯ ⎯ ⎯ ⎯ ⎯ ⎯ winter Olympic event

7. ⎯ ⎯ ⎯ ⎯ ⎯ speed skaters ride on these

8. ⎯ ⎯ ◯ ⎯ ⎯ lugers want as little as possible

9. ⎯ ⎯ ◯ ⎯ ⎯ ⎯ an athlete's most important piece of equipment

Unscramble the letters in the circles to find the clue word.

⎯ h ⎯ ⎯ ⎯ ⎯ ⎯ ⎯ part of the early Olympics

SPEED RACE

What a Rush!

Luge is the French word for "sled." A luge can reach up to 130 km/hr (about 80 mi/hr). A luge is designed to whisk down mountains of ice with as little resistance as possible. A luge is made of fiberglass with blades attached to each side. These blades are the only part of the luge that comes in contact with the ice. Lugers polish the blades to reduce friction as they speed down the icy course. The blades are bowed, or bent, allowing only about 2.5 cm (about 1 in.) to come into contact with the ice at one time. After takeoff, lugers lie down on their backs, feet first, to steer, directing the luge through the curved, icy track by slight shifts of their body weight.

Dragging Your Feet

Tobogganing is another popular Olympic sport. Did you know that toboggans can go up to 145 km/hr (about 90 mi/hr)? Some of the first toboggans were sleds made out of bark and skin. Today, the front end of a toboggan is curled back for going over bumps, and the flat bottom is waxed for swift motion. To change direction, a rider must shift his or her weight.

— Fold —

MOMENTUM MACHINE

An ice skater goes into a spin. Suddenly the spinning becomes faster and faster. Why the sudden change?

MATERIALS

▶ rotating stool or chair   ▶ 2 bricks or hand weights

PROCEDURE

1. Sit on the stool with a brick in each hand. Hold your arms out away from your body.

2. Have your partner begin to rotate you slowly. Then tell your partner to let go and move away.

3. Quickly pull the bricks to your chest. What did you notice? CAUTION: **spinning very rapidly may upset the stool. You may also be dizzy when you get up.**

4. Repeat the experiment. Then trade places with your partner.

CONCLUSIONS

You might want to try the experiment again. This time begin with your arms at your chest and then extend them outward. How does this change your speed of rotation?

REASONS TO LOVE YOUR TOES

Did you know that feet are the most important piece of equipment any athlete can have? Feet serve as launching pads, shock absorbers, pivots, levers, propellers, and grippers. Footwork is literally the foundation of most sports.

According to foot experts who study sports performance, if your big toe extends farther than your middle toe, you have a natural advantage in sports such as skiing, sprinting, and the long jump. People with long big toes are able to lean their full body weight onto the area of the foot that allows them to accelerate quickly.

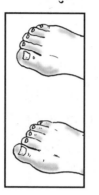

Think & Do

Stand next to a wall. Make a mark on it where your hand touches when you extend your arm all the way above your head. Then try jumping. Mark the height of your jump. Try it again, but this time, bend your knees a little more. Did you jump higher? Why?

LET THE GAMES BEGIN!

Did you know that the first Olympic games in 776 B.C. were part of an ancient Greek religious festival? In the beginning, only men were allowed to compete in and to watch the games. The only event in the first 13 Olympic games was a footrace of about 180 m (about 200 yd). The four-horse chariot race was added in 680 B.C. In A.D. 394, the games ended. They were said to have lost their religious meaning because the competitors cared only about winning money. The games weren't held again for more than 1500 years.

The Modern Olympics

An earthquake destroyed the Stadium of Olympia around A.D. 500, and a landslide later buried what was left of the structure. Imagine the excitement of the team of archaeologists who discovered the ruins in 1875! The discovery led to the resumption of the games. The first modern Olympic games took place in 1896.

Find Out

Look up the Olympics in an encyclopedia. What sorts of games did the ancient Greeks enjoy? How have the Olympics changed over the years? What are the newest Olympic events?

Fold

SATELLITES IN ORBIT

FAST FACT

What do you think takes more thrust—moving forward or moving upward? In order to defy gravity and boost a satellite into space, a rocket ship must fly more than 24,000 km/hr (about 15,000 mi/hr).

FAST FACT

Artificial satellites used for navigation can pinpoint the exact location of a ship on the ocean.

FAST FACT

Ganymede, one of Jupiter's moons, is the largest natural satellite known to humans. It is bigger than Mercury and has oxygen in its atmosphere.

Fold

Science Fun

New Launch

NASA has plans to launch a satellite called the *IMAGE* into orbit soon. *IMAGE* is designed to provide information on an invisible force— No, not THE FORCE— Earth's invisible magnetosphere. Earth is surrounded by a cloud of ionized gas that protects it from solar radiation. With the cameras mounted on *IMAGE*, scientists will be able to view the magnetosphere from both the inside and the outside as *IMADE'S* orbit carries it in a loop pattern around Earth.

RIDDLES TO SEND YOU INTO ORBIT

▲ 1. How does the man in the moon eat his dinner?
▲ 2. Why is a satellite like a gossip?
▲ 3. What did the satellite say when the music slowed down and a lot of questionable characters drifted by?
▲ 4. What do you call a fast-paced city?
▲ 5. Why did the moon enter its orbit in the dog show?
▲ 6. How did the moon show it was sorry for being so distant?
▲ 7. How did the scientist explain his fear that the satellite would fall?

Answers to Vocabulary Fun: boost; gravity; signals; sun; atmospheric drag; satellite dish.
Answers to Science Fun: 1. out of a satellite dish. 2. It circles the globe and repeats whatever it hears. 3. "Hey, this is an atmospheric drag." 4. Velocity. 5. It had an official perigee (pedigree). 6. It offered an apogee (apology). 7. with gravity

Harcourt

GRAVITY
MAY THE FORCE BE WITH YOU

The force of gravity causes apples to drop off trees and water to run downhill. It also keeps moons, planets, suns, and artificial satellites in orbit. A satellite is an object that moves in an orbit around a larger heavenly body. There are two kinds of satellites—natural satellites and artificial satellites.

Satellites stay in orbit for a simple reason. An object in orbit around the Earth is moving forward and falling toward Earth at the same time. If it is moving forward fast enough, it will never land on Earth. This is due to the curvature of the Earth. When you spin a rock around you on a string, the rock swings toward your hand without ever touching your hand as long as you whirl it fast enough. In a similar way, satellites always fall toward the objects they orbit without ever landing on them.

This is how shuttles stay in orbit. The shuttle is launched into a path that arcs above the Earth, traveling parallel to Earth's surface at sufficient speed. The speed of the orbiter is determined by the distance from Earth's surface.

Fold

Vocabulary Fun

A Satellite Story

Help tell this story about a satellite by filling in the blanks below with words chosen from this list.

sun	signals	satellite dish
atmospheric drag	boost	gravity

Two kids were walking down the street one day. They met a scientist who said he had just invented a new satellite. He needed their help to get it into orbit. He said, "In order to (1) _____ my satellite into space, I need a rocket ship that can fly more than 24,000 km/hr (about 15,000 mi/hr)."

"Why, you can't go that fast," they said. "Are you trying to break the law?"

"Only the law of (2) _____," he said. "And I also need a giant spaghetti bowl. Do you have one at your house?"

"Yes, but our mother might miss it. What is it for?"

"To pick up the (3) _____ my satellite sends."

"How will your satellite get power?" the kids asked.

"I can harness the power of the (4) _____," he said.

"Well, why do you have to go so fast?"

"To avoid (5) _____. It's a real drag, you know. Now what about the loan?"

"Let's go get the bowl," the kids cried. "We'll have the first spaghetti bowl-sized (6) _____ in history!"

Answers on page 8

Harcour

NATURAL SATELLITES

Many Moons

Naturally occurring satellites are called *moons*. While humans make satellites out of various metals and electric parts, nature makes satellites out of floating objects in space.

Scientists don't really know how long our moon has orbited Earth or just where it came from. It might be a part of Earth that broke off, or it might be a large meteor that was trapped in Earth's gravitational pull. Early civilizations used myths and legends to explain the moon's appearance each night.

While Earth's gravity keeps the moon in orbit, the moon's gravity controls the ocean tides. Think about what the ocean would look like if the moon's gravity did not pull it outward.

The moon's orbit is an *ellipse*, or oval, rather than a perfect circle. The point in the orbit where the moon is closest to Earth is called the *perigee*. The moon's perigee is 357,274 km (about 222,000 mi) from Earth. The point where the moon swings farthest away from Earth is the *apogee*. The moon's apogee lies 53,108 km (about 33,000 mi) farther from Earth than its perigee.

— Fold —

IN ORBIT

Use this model to see how satellites orbit Earth.

MATERIALS

▲ tennis ball
▲ 2 m of string
▲ flower pot
▲ large ball (or globe)
▲ knife

PROCEDURE

1. Ask an adult to cut a small slit in the tennis ball for you. Tie a knot in one end of the string. Squeeze the slit open. Insert the knotted end into the slit in the ball.

2. Set the large ball in the open end of the flower pot. Place the pot and the ball in the center of a clear space. One person should hold the string with the tennis ball so that the string hangs directly over the north pole of the large ball and the small ball is even with the large ball's equator.

3. While one person holds the string steady, the second person should start the ball moving. The goal is to move the small ball into orbit around the large ball.

CONCLUSIONS

Why did you need to hold the small ball away from the large ball before sending it into orbit? What happened if the ball moved too slowly? Did the distance of the small ball from the large ball affect the need for speed?

ARTIFICIAL SATELLITES
Far Out

Hundreds of artificial satellites orbit Earth. Many of them stay in orbit for decades. You might think that some of these satellites would hit each other, but they are carefully positioned with a lot of space between their orbits.

The United States uses space shuttles to send satellites into orbit. A satellite must reach a height at least 160 km (about 100 mi) above Earth's surface. At this height it is low enough to respond to Earth's gravity, but high enough to almost leave the atmosphere. If it is too low, objects in the atmosphere will slow it down, creating a condition called *atmospheric drag*. If you tried swinging the rock on the string, you know why a satellite cannot slow down too much. Once in orbit the satellite must travel at a speed of 28,300 km/hr (about 17,585 mi/hr) to maintain orbit.

ORBIT WITH A PURPOSE
Reach Way Out and Touch Someone

Have you ever talked with someone in another country or on a different continent? Artificial satellites transmit communication signals that let people from every corner of the globe keep in touch with one another. They also let us watch events in faraway places as they happen. Artificial satellites are also used for the following:

- as space stations and astronomical observatories.
- for taking pictures of Earth and things in outer space.
- for ocean navigation.
- for surveying, crop forecasting, flood control, mineral exploration, land management, and reforestation.
- to gather information for the military.
- to monitor the weather worldwide.

Find Out

Learn more about *Sputnik I*, the very first artificial satellite. It was launched by the Soviet Union on October 4, 1957.

LASER BEAMS

Fold

Harcourt

Science Fun

LASER RIDDLES

▶ 1. How can you tell when a laser has died?

▶ 2. What did the laser do to make a great impression at the potato chip company?

▶ 3. How can you tell when lasers are really happy?

"Stop, Everyone Is Talking at Once!"

Suppose you are talking with a friend in another country. Telephone links rely on small lasers to send signals through many miles of fiber-optic cable. Some of these cables run under the sea. A single beam can carry up to hundreds of thousands of telephone calls!

Have Fun with Lasers

A new game has been developed using lasers. It's called laser tag. Just like the game of tag, it involves seeking an opponent. Each team member wears a special vest and carries a laser beam. The goal is to touch the laser beam to your opponent's vest before he or she can tag you. When the vest you are wearing emits a beep, you've been tagged.

Answers to Vocabulary Fun: *Laser* stands for light amplification stimulated emission radiation. 1. hologram, 2. pulse, 3. dimension.

Answers to Science Fun: 1. It doesn't have a pulse. 2. It was very appealing (a-peeling). 3. They are beaming!

VocabularyFun

3-D Word Puzzle

Write the word for which each letter in this acronym stands. Copy the letters that have a shape next to them onto the correct lines that follow. Then unscramble the letters to find three words that relate to lasers.

L(□)   A   S   E(□)   R(○)

1. ___ ___ ___ ___ ___ (circles)
2. ___ ___ ___ ___ ___ (squares)
3. ___ ___ ___ ___ ___ ___ (triangles)

Abbreviate yourself! Turn your name into an abbreviation. Think of words that describe YOU, starting with each letter of your name!

Answers on page 8
Take-Home Book • 7

LASER IS LIGHT

The word *laser* stands for *light amplification by stimulated emission of radiation*. Unlike light from the sun or a lamp that spreads out in all directions, lasers are very strong, focused rays of light that project in a very narrow path. Unlike other light waves, laser light waves are all in the same phase.

Moving Pictures

Even though a laser looks like a continuous ray of light, it is actually a beam that flashes 12,000 times per second! Because the pulses are so fast, the human eye sees a straight line. In the same way, movies are a series of still photographs that we see as many moving images.

Music to Your Ears

You've seen CD players. Did you know that laser technology made it possible for CDs to replace those vinyl records your parents danced to? CDs translate sound waves into numbers, or digits. These digits, which are stored in microscopic grooves on the compact disc, are read by a beam of laser light as the disc turns. The reflected light is turned into an electric signal before it becomes the music that we hear. When you stop to think about it, in a way what we are hearing is light!

2 • Take-Home Book

Fold

LASERS HELP DOCTORS

In the past 30 years, many uses of lasers have been developed. The area in which lasers have benefited people the most is medicine.

Dentists use lasers to detect cavities and remove stains from teeth. Surgeons and doctors use lasers to do the following:

- remove skin growths.
- correct imperfect vision.
- cure certain eye diseases.
- erase scars.
- remove tattoos.
- smooth wrinkles.
- treat heart disease, hearing loss, and muscle pain.

Lasers Make a Difference

In some cases, lasers have been able to prevent total blindness. Because they are so powerful and precise, lasers are also used to remove small groups of cells before they become cancerous, leaving the surrounding healthy cells unaffected.

— Fold —

BEAM ME UP, SCOTTY!

How close can a human being come to duplicating the speed at which a laser pulses?

MATERIALS

▲ notebook ▲ pencil
▲ light switch ▲ stopwatch

PROCEDURE

1. In order to understand just how false light pulses in a laser beam, stand next to a light switch on the wall and flick it on and off. Time yourself. In the space of one second, see if you can turn it off and on 12,000 times!

2. Write down how many times you were actually able to flick the switch in one second. Divide that number into 12,000 in order to find out how many seconds it would take you to do what a laser can do in one.

CONCLUSIONS

From what you now know, what other things do you think lasers might be used for? Make a list of the possibilities. Be creative. Could we use lasers to brush our teeth? Could they clean dirt from under our nails? Could we use them instead of scissors? Why or why not?

LASERS ARE EVERYWHERE

Lasers even make it easier to catch criminals! They are often used in crime laboratories to find fingerprints on surfaces, such as glass, paper, wood, and skin, that other methods cannot detect.

Geophysicists use lasers to measure the movement of Earth's crustal plains in order to predict future earthquakes. Lasers are also used to monitor fault lines, such as the San Andreas fault in California.

Lasers are used in security systems to prevent robberies. In these systems, an invisible laser beam crosses a door or window. If someone crosses the beam, an alarm goes off and the police come.

Sound and light shows use lasers to produce animated images on screens. Holograms, or three-dimensional images, are also formed with the aid of lasers. Have you been on the haunted-house ride at Disneyland? Did you see yourself sitting next to a ghost? You weren't really afraid of a simple beam of light, were you?

Fold

A BRIGHT FUTURE

Right now scientists are busy developing lots of new uses for lasers. Someday, instead of watching flat television screens, people might sit across from three-dimensional holographic characters in their favorite programs while the program goes on around them. Some people think that advances in CDs may soon make books made from paper obsolete.

NASA is already using lasers to map the surfaces of other planets, such as Mars. Oceanographers use lasers to map the ocean floor. Who knows what we will be able to do with the aid of new and improved lasers?

Think & Do

Make a list of all the lasers you come in contact with every day. Don't forget the lasers in grocery stores and libraries! How many other "everyday" lasers can you think of?

ELECTRIC VEHICLES

Harcourt

FAST FACT

It is estimated that about 30 million electric vehicles in the United States could be recharged without constructing even one new power plant.

FAST FACT

The United States is the world's largest oil consumer, using about 1772 million tons of oil a year.

Fold

Science Fun

GOT ANY KETCHUP?

People have experimented with many strange ways of fueling their cars. A Florida man, for example, converted his car engine to use vegetable oil, which he collected from fast-food restaurant trash bins. Observers said that although the man's car seemed to run well, the exhaust smelled a lot like French fries.

Read More About Electric Cars!

- *Green Cars: Earth-Friendly Electric Vehicles* by John Coughlan

- For more information about the Gizmo, visit the Neighborhood Electric Vehicle Company Web site at www.nevco.com

IT'S ECONOMICAL, RUNS GREAT, AND DOESN'T POLLUTE BUT THE CORD ONLY LETS ME RUN AROUND THE BLOCK A COUPLE OF TIMES!

Answers to Vocabulary Fun: 1. fossil fuel, 2. quiet, 3. recharge, 4. Ford, 5. inexpensive, 6. Gizmo, 7. electric, 8. gasoline, 9. nonpolluting.

ELECTRIC CARS

Do you think electric vehicles (EVs) are new? Guess again. The first-known electric car was built by a Dutchman in 1835. The first practical electric road vehicle was introduced seven years later, in 1842. The main problem for these early inventors was the battery, which was nonrechargeable. In 1865, the storage battery was invented. It was improved in 1881. This was good news for the electric-car builders. By 1899, electric cars were the rage. In 1899, an electric car was the first car to travel faster than 100 km/hr (about 62 mi/hr). But these cars were expensive and so was electricity. In fact, electricity was not readily available. People didn't appreciate traveling to a place by car and then not being able to make the return trip because the battery had run down. But for around town, the electric car was the best to be had.

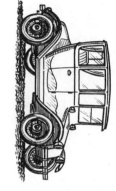

Henry Ford put an end to the era of the electric car with his gas-powered Model T Ford. By 1925, Ford had already manufactured 10 million cars, and, because he charged a mere $260, more people were able to buy his cars than could afford their electric counterparts. And ways to make gasoline cheaply had already been developed. As a result, gasoline was readily available in many parts of the country.

2 • **Take-Home Book**

Fold

Harcourt

VocabularyFun

It All Started With the Wheel

Unscramble the vocabulary words in each wheel.

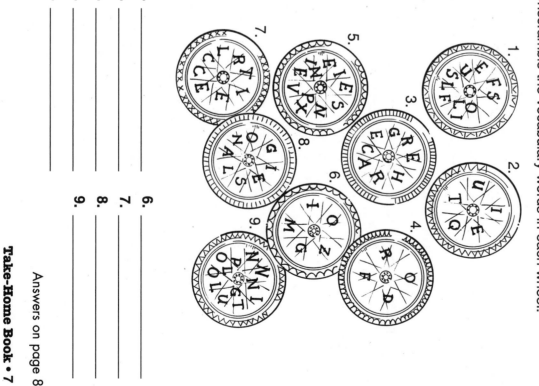

1. _____
2. _____
3. _____
4. _____
5. _____
6. _____
7. _____
8. _____
9. _____

Answers on page 8

NOW, IMAGINE THIS SCENE

Your parents get up, plug in the coffee pot, and unplug their EVs. They head off to work in vehicles that are quiet, non-polluting, and cheap to operate. Then, when it's time to pile in some of the soccer team for an out-of-town game, you use the minivan.

Gizmos®—A New Vision

Many automobile companies are working on electric-vehicle designs. Mark Murphy, of the Neighborhood Electric Vehicle Company (NEVC), is taking a unique approach with the development of the Gizmo. Gizmos and other EVs like it may be an inexpensive and practical solution to most of the driving people do in town.

It also makes sense. At 65 km/hr (about 40 mi/hr), EVs go as fast as most people go in town. They don't use gasoline, and they're easy to park. Gizmos can only go about 30 km (about 20 mi) before they have to be recharged, but most neighborhood trips are shorter than this. Murphy believes when the Gizmo starts production, it could sell for about $5000 and only cost about $0.01 per mile for the electricity.

Fold

YOUR FAMILY'S DRIVING HABITS

What are your family's driving habits? Enlist the help of family members to find out.

MATERIALS

▲ notebook
▲ survey sheet
▲ pencil
▲ a sheet of large graph paper

PROCEDURE

Keep a notebook and pencil in your family's car (or cars) for two weeks. Ask all family members who drive to write down the number of miles they drive every time they use the car.

• What was the shortest trip made in one day? The longest trip?

• What was the average number of miles driven per day during these two weeks?

• How many times did a family member drive more than 30 miles? Less than 30 miles? Less than 15 miles?

At the end of the month, make a graph of your data that looks like this:

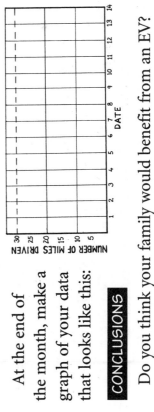

CONCLUSIONS

Do you think your family would benefit from an EV? Why or why not?

DISTANCE RUNNERS

EVs are not like the Energizer Bunny®, "which keeps going, and going, and going." In electric cars the batteries run down and have to be recharged by plugging the car into an electric outlet. In 1995 the Solectria Sunrise set a record for battery endurance. This EV traveled 383 km (about 238 mi) on one charge. Scientists are hoping that by the year 2001 a standard EV will be able to travel 160 to 320 km (about 100 to 200 mi) before needing a recharge.

Future for EVs

California is leading the way in converting to EVs. Government officials have stated that by the year 2003, one of every ten cars sold in that state will be electric-powered. But the state is not just waiting for private citizens to convert. It has already taken big steps. Yosemite National Park has two new electric tour buses. These are quiet buses with no diesel fumes to foul the air, and they cost less to run than the old gasoline-powered buses. California already has trolleys, city buses, trains, and even school buses that are powered by electricity.

Think & Do

Research electric-car designs. Then make some sketches of your own. Which designs do you like best, and why?

ELECTRIC BICYCLE

Need practical transportation for short errands and jaunts around town? Try an electric bicycle. An electric bicycle is lightweight, quick, and safe. It looks like a regular bike, but it has a small motor and there is a pouch hanging below the seat. That is where the battery for the EV is mounted. There is a trailer available for the bike, so if you are on your way to the grocery and end up buying more than just milk, never fear. You can carry 45 kg (about 100 lb) and still travel 24 km/hr (about 15 mi/hr) for almost 8 km (about 5 mi). The good thing about this vehicle is the cost. For just a little less than $1000, you could have your very own electric vehicle.

Find Out

Stand on a busy street corner with two friends between 4:00 P.M. and 5:00 P.M. on a weekday afternoon. Count the number of cars that pass with one person in them. Have a friend keep track of the number of big utility vehicles, pickups, and minivans. Have the other friend count the total number of vehicles. Then compare notes. What did you learn from your short survey?